Abandonment to Divine Providence

Jean-Pierre de Caussade

DOVER PUBLICATIONS, INC.
Mineola, New York

Bibliographical Note

This Dover edition, first published in 2008, is a newly reset, unabridged republication of Books I and II from *Abandonment to Divine Providence* by Jean-Pierre de Caussade, from the Tenth Complete French Edition by E. J. Strickland, edited by the Rev. J. Ramière, and originally published by B. Herder Book Company, St. Louis, Mo., in 1921.

The original introduction, written by Dom Arnold, has been modified for the present edition. Only those paragraphs that directly pertain to Father de Caussade's book on *Abandonment to Divine Providence* have been reprinted here.

Library of Congress Cataloging-in-Publication Data

Caussade, Jean Pierre de, d. 1751.
    [Abandon à la providence divine. English]
    Abandonment to divine providence / Jean-Pierre de Caussade. — Dover ed.
       p. cm.
    Originally published: St. Louis, MO : B. Herder Book Co., 1921.
    ISBN-13: 978-0-486-46426-8
    ISBN-10: 0-486-46426-1
    1. Mysticism—Catholic Church. 2. Spiritual life—Catholic Church. I. Title.

BV5082.3.C3813 2008
248.2'2—dc22

2007046754

Manufactured in the United States of America
Dover Publications, Inc., 31 East 2nd Street, Mineola, N.Y. 11501

INTRODUCTION

The Rev. Jean-Pierre de Caussade was one of the most remarkable spiritual writers of the Society of Jesus in France in the 18th century. His death took place at Toulouse in 1751. His works have gone through many editions and have been republished and translated into several foreign languages.

This edition (1921) gives an English translation of the tenth French Edition of Fr. de Caussade's *Abandon à la Providence Divine,* edited, to the great benefit of many souls, by Fr. H. Ramière, S. J. The 1921 edition is divided into two distinct parts—the first contains a theoretical treatise on total abandonment to Divine Providence, and the second, letters of direction for persons leading a spiritual life.*

The "Treatise" comprises two different aspects of Abandonment to Divine Providence; one as a *virtue,* common and necessary to all Christians, the other as a state, proper to souls who have made a special practice of abandonment to the holy will of God.

The "Abandonment to Divine Providence" of Fr. de Caussade is as far removed from the false inactivity of the Quietists, as true Christian resignation is distinct from the fatalism of Mohammedans. It is a trusting, childlike, peaceful abandonment to the guidance of grace, and of the Holy Spirit: an unquestioning and undoubting submission to the holy will of God in all things that may befall us, be they due to the action of man, or to the direct permission of God. To Fr. de Caussade, abandonment to God, the "Ita Pater" of our Divine Lord, the "Fiat" of our Blessed Lady, is the shortest, surest, and easiest

---

*The present volume reprints the complete contents of the first portion.

way to holiness and peace. Fr. de Caussade's work must be read with a certain amount of discretion, as naturally every advice he gives does not apply to all readers indiscriminately. Some of his counsels may be appropriate for beginners; others for souls of a more advanced degree of spirituality. No one, however, can fail to recognise in his writings the sure tone of a "Master," who has united practical to theoretical knowledge of his subject.

Every page is redolent with the unction of the Spirit of God, and readers will find in his doctrine a heavenly manna, a food of unfailing strength for their souls. The present work has been carefully translated into readable English, and more regard has been paid to the meaning than to the literal exactness of the sentences. The elevated, noble style of the author has been preserved throughout. It is a real contribution to the spiritual literature of England.

I am aware that our English word "Abandonment" does not adequately render the meaning of the French word "Abandon," but we have no better expression. The translation has been undertaken solely for the purpose of helping souls to follow the hidden paths of the spiritual life, and to surrender themselves entirely to the guidance of the Holy Spirit.

Dom Arnold, O.S.B.
Buckfast Abbey

(Feast of All Saints, 1921.)

Contents

BOOK I

ON THE VIRTUE OF ABANDONMENT TO DIVINE PROVIDENCE;
ITS NATURE AND EXCELLENCE.

CHAPTER I

SANCTITY CONSISTS IN FIDELITY TO THE ORDER OF GOD,
AND IN SUBMISSION TO ALL HIS OPERATIONS.

CHAPTER II

THE DIVINE ACTION WORKS UNCEASINGLY
FOR THE SANCTIFICATION OF SOULS.

BOOK II

CHAPTER I

ON THE NATURE AND EXCELLENCE
OF THE STATE OF ABANDONMENT.

CHAPTER II

THE DUTIES OF THOSE SOULS CALLED BY GOD
TO THE STATE OF ABANDONMENT.

CHAPTER III

THE TRIALS CONNECTED WITH THE STATE OF ABANDONMENT.

CHAPTER IV

CONCERNING THE ASSISTANCE RENDERED
BY THE FATHERLY PROVIDENCE OF GOD TO THOSE SOULS
WHO HAVE ABANDONED THEMSELVES TO HIM.

BOOK I

ON THE VIRTUE OF ABANDONMENT TO DIVINE
PROVIDENCE; ITS NATURE AND EXCELLENCE

CHAPTER I.

SECTION I.—*Hidden Operations of God.*

Fidelity to the order established by God comprehended the whole sanctity of the righteous under the old law; even that of St. Joseph, and of Mary herself.

God continues to speak to-day as He spoke in former times to our fathers when there were no directors as at present, nor any regular method of direction. Then all spirituality was comprised in fidelity to the designs of God, for there was no regular system of guidance in the spiritual life to explain it in detail, nor so many instructions, precepts and examples as there are now. Doubtless our present difficulties render this necessary, but it was not so in the first ages when souls were more simple and straightforward. Then, for those who led a spiritual life, each moment brought some duty to be faithfully accomplished. Their whole attention was thus concentrated consecutively like a hand that marks the hours which, at each moment, traverses the space allotted to it. Their minds, incessantly animated by the impulsion of divine grace, turned imperceptibly to each new duty that presented itself by the permission of God at different hours of the day. Such were the hidden springs by which the conduct of Mary was actuated. Mary was the most simple of all creatures, and the most closely united to God. Her answer to the angel when she said: "Fiat mihi secundum verbum tuum": contained all the mystic theology of her ancestors to whom everything was reduced, as it is now, to the purest, simplest

submission of the soul to the will of God, under whatever form
it presents itself. This beautiful and exalted state, which was the
basis of the spiritual life of Mary, shines conspicuously in these
simple words, "Fiat mihi" (Luke i, 38). Take notice that they are
in complete harmony with those which Our Lord desires that
we should have always on our lips and in our hearts: "Fiat vol-
untas tua." It is true that what was required of Mary at this great
moment, was for her very great glory, but the magnificence of
this glory would have made no impression on her if she had not
seen in it the fulfilment of the will of God. In all things was she
ruled by the divine will. Were her occupations ordinary, or of an
elevated nature, they were to her but the manifestation, sometimes obscure, sometimes clear, of the operations of the most
High, in which she found alike subject matter for the glory of
God. Her spirit, transported with joy, looked upon all that she
had to do or to suffer at each moment as the gift of Him who
fills with good things the hearts of those who hunger and thirst
for Him alone, and have no desire for created things.

SECTION II.—*The Hidden Operations of God, continued*

The duties of each moment are the shadows beneath which
hides the divine operation.

"The power of the most High shall over-shadow thee" (Luke
i, 35), said the angel to Mary. This shadow, beneath which is
hidden the power of God for the purpose of bringing forth Jesus
Christ in the soul, is the duty, the attraction, or the cross that is
presented to us at each moment. These are, in fact, but shadows
like those in the order of nature which, like a veil, cover sensible
objects and hide them from us. Therefore in the moral and
supernatural order the duties of each moment conceal, under
the semblance of dark shadows, the truth of their divine character which alone should rivet the attention. It was in this light
that Mary beheld them. Also these shadows diffused over her
faculties, far from creating illusion, did but increase her faith in
Him who is unchanging and unchangeable. The archangel may
depart. He has delivered his message, and his moment has

passed. Mary advances without ceasing, and is already far beyond him. The Holy Spirit, who comes to take possession of her under the shadow of the angel's words, will never abandon her.

There are remarkably few extraordinary characteristics in the outward events of the life of the most holy Virgin, at least there are none recorded in holy Scripture. Her exterior life is represented as very ordinary and simple. She did and suffered the same things that anyone in a similar state of life might do or suffer. She goes to visit her cousin Elizabeth as her other relatives did. She took shelter in a stable in consequence of her poverty. She returned to Nazareth from whence she had been driven by the persecution of Herod, and lived there with Jesus and Joseph, supporting themselves by the work of their hands. It was in this way that the holy family gained their daily bread. But what a divine nourishment Mary and Joseph received from this daily bread for the strengthening of their faith! It is like a sacrament to sanctify all their moments. What treasures of grace lie concealed in these moments filled, apparently, by the most ordinary events. That which is visible might happen to anyone, but the invisible, discerned by faith, is no less than God operating very great things. O Bread of Angels! heavenly manna! pearl of the Gospel! Sacrament of the present moment! thou givest God under as lowly a form as the manger, the hay, or the straw. And to whom dost thou give Him? "Esurientes implevit bonis" (Luke i, 53). God reveals Himself to the humble under the most lowly forms, but the proud, attaching themselves entirely to that which is extrinsic, do not discover Him hidden beneath, and are sent empty away.

SECTION III.—*The Work of our Sanctification.*

How much more easily sanctity appears when regarded from this point of view.

If the work of our sanctification presents, apparently, the most insurmountable difficulties, it is because we do not know how to form a just idea of it. In reality sanctity can be reduced to one single practice, fidelity to the duties appointed by God. Now this fidelity is equally within each one's power whether in its active practice, or passive exercise.

The active practice of fidelity consists in accomplishing the duties which devolve upon us whether imposed by the general laws of God and of the Church, or by the particular state that we may have embraced. Its passive exercise consists in the loving acceptance of all that God sends us at each moment.

Are either of these practices of sanctity above our strength? Certainly not the active fidelity, since the duties it imposes cease to be duties when we have no longer the power to fulfil them. If the state of your health does not permit you to go to Mass you are not obliged to go. The same rule holds good for all the precepts laid down; that is to say for all those which prescribe certain duties. Only those which forbid things evil in themselves are absolute, because it is never allowable to commit sin. Can there, then, be anything more reasonable? What excuse can be made? Yet this is all that God requires of the soul for the work of its sanctification. He exacts it from both high and low, from the strong and the weak, in a word from all, always and everywhere. It is true then that He requires on our part only simple and easy things since it is only necessary to employ this simple method to attain to an eminent degree of sanctity. If, over and above the Commandments, He shows us the counsels as a more perfect aim, He always takes care to suit the practice of them to our position and character. He bestows on us, as the principal sign of our vocation to follow them, the attractions of grace which make them easy. He never impels anyone beyond his strength, nor in any way beyond his aptitude. Again, what could be more just? All you who strive after perfection and who are tempted to discouragement at the remembrance of what you have read in the lives of the saints, and of what certain pious books prescribe; O you who are appalled by the terrible ideas of perfection that you have formed for yourselves; it is for your consolation that God has willed me to write this. Learn that of which you seem to be ignorant. This God of all goodness has made those things easy which are common and necessary in the order of nature, such as breathing, eating, and sleeping. No less

necessary in the supernatural order are love and fidelity, therefore it must needs be that the difficulty of acquiring them is by
no means so great as is generally represented. Review your life.
Is it not composed of innumerable actions of very little importance? Well, God is quite satisfied with these. They are the
share that the soul must take in the work of its perfection. This
is so clearly explained in Holy Scripture that there can be no
doubt about it: "Fear God and keep the commandments, this is
the whole duty of man" (Ecclesiastes xii, 13), that is to say—this
is all that is required on the part of man, and it is in this that
active fidelity consists. If man fulfils his part God will do the
rest. Grace being bestowed only on this condition the marvels it
effects are beyond the comprehension of man. For neither ear
has heard nor eye seen, nor has it entered the mind what things
God has planned in His omniscience, determined in His will,
and carried out by His power in the souls given up entirely to
Him. The passive part of sanctity is still more easy since it only
consists in accepting that which we very often have no power to
prevent, and in suffering lovingly, that is to say with sweetness
and consolation, those things that too often cause weariness and
disgust. Once more I repeat, in this consists sanctity. This is the
grain of mustard seed which is the smallest of all the seeds, the
fruits of which can neither be recognised nor gathered. It is
the drachma of the Gospel, the treasure that none discover
because they suppose it to be too far away to be sought. Do not
ask me how this treasure can be found. It is no secret. The treasure is everywhere, it is offered to us at all times and wherever
we may be. All creatures, both friends and enemies pour it out
with prodigality, and it flows like a fountain through every faculty of body and soul even to the very centre of our hearts. If we
open our mouths they will be filled. The divine activity perme-
ates the whole universe, it pervades every creature; wherever
they are it is there; it goes before them, with them, and it follows
them; all they have to do is to let the waves bear them on.

    Would to God that kings and their ministers, princes of the
Church and of the world, priests and soldiers, the peasantry and
labourers, in a word, all men could know how very easy it would
be for them to arrive at a high degree of sanctity. They would

only have to fulfil the simple duties of Christianity and of their state of life; to embrace with submission the crosses belonging to that state, and to submit with faith and love to the designs of Providence in all those things that have to be done or suffered without going out of their way to seek occasions for themselves. This is the spirit by which the patriarchs and prophets were animated and sanctified before there were so many systems of so many masters of the spiritual life.° This is the spirituality of all ages and of every state. No state of life can, assuredly, be sanctified in a more exalted manner, nor in a more wonderful and easy way than by the simple use of the means that God, the sovereign director of souls, gives them to do or to suffer at each moment.

SECTION IV.—*In what Perfection Consists.*

Perfection consists in doing the will of God, not in understanding His designs.

The designs of God, the good pleasure of God, the will of God, the operation of God and the gift of His grace are all one and the same thing in the spiritual life. It is God working in the soul to make it like unto Himself. Perfection is neither more nor less than the faithful co-operation of the soul with this work of God, and is begun, grows, and is consummated in the soul unperceived and in secret. The science of theology is full of theories and explanations of the wonders of this state in each soul according to its capacity. One may be conversant with all these speculations, speak and write about them admirably,

---

°It would be a mistaken idea of the meaning of the author to imagine that he would urge anyone to undertake to lead a spiritual life without the guidance of a director. He explains expressly elsewhere that in order to be able to do without a director one must have been habitually and for a long time under direction. Less still does he endeavour to bring into disrepute the means made use of by the Church for the extirpation of vice and the acquisition of virtue. His meaning, of which Christians cannot be too often reminded, is, that of all direction the best is that of divine Providence, and that the most necessary and the most sanctifying of all practices is that of fulfilling faithfully and accepting lovingly whatever this paternal Providence ordains that we should do or suffer.

instruct others and guide souls; yet, if these theories are only in the mind, one is, compared with those who, without any knowledge of these theories, receive the meaning of the designs of God and do His holy will, like a sick physician compared to simple people in perfect health. The designs of God and his divine will accepted by a faithful soul with simplicity produces this divine state in it without its knowledge, just as a medicine taken obediently will produce health, although the sick person neither knows nor wishes to know anything about medicine. As fire gives out heat, and not philosophical discussions about it, nor knowledge of its effects, so the designs of God and His holy will work in the soul for its sanctification, and not speculations of curiosity as to this principle and this state. When one is thirsty one quenches one's thirst by drinking, not by reading books which treat of this condition. The desire to know does but increase this thirst. Therefore when one thirsts after sanctity, the desire to know about it only drives it further away. Speculation must be laid aside, and everything arranged by God as regards actions and sufferings must be accepted with simplicity, for those things that happen at each moment by the divine command or permission are always the most holy, the best and the most divine for us.

SECTION V.—*The Divine Influence alone can Sanctify Us.*

No reading, nor any other exercise can sanctify us except in so far as they are the channels of the divine influence.

Our whole science consists in recognising the designs of God for the present moment. All reading not intended for us by God is dangerous. It is by doing the will of God and obeying His holy inspirations that we obtain grace, and this grace works in our hearts through our reading or any other employment. Apart from God reading is empty and vain and, being deprived for us of the life-giving power of the action of God, only succeeds in emptying the heart by the very fullness it gives to the mind.

This divine will, working in the soul of a simple ignorant girl by means of sufferings and actions of a very ordinary nature, produces a state of supernatural life without the mind being filled with self-exalting ideas; whereas the proud man who studies spiritual books merely out of curiosity receives no more than the dead letter into his mind, and the will of God having no connexion with his reading his heart becomes ever harder and more withered.

The order established by God and His divine will are the life of the soul no matter in what way they work, or are obeyed. Whatever connexion the divine will has with the mind, it nourishes the soul, and continually enlarges it by giving it what is best for it at every moment. It is neither one thing nor another which produces these happy effects, but what God has willed for each moment. What was best for the moment that has passed is so no longer because it is no longer the will of God which, becoming apparent through other circumstances, brings to light the duty of the present moment. It is this duty under whatever guise it presents itself which is precisely that which is the most sanctifying for the soul. If, by the divine will, it is a present duty to read, then reading will produce the destined effect in the soul. If it is the divine will that reading be relinquished for contemplation, then this will perform the work of God in the soul and reading would become useless and prejudicial. Should the divine will withdraw the soul from contemplation for the hearing of confessions, etc., and that even for some considerable time, this duty becomes the means of uniting the soul with Jesus Christ and all the sweetness of contemplation would only serve to destroy this union. Our moments are made fruitful by our fulfilment of the will of God. This is presented to us in countless different ways by the present duty which forms, increases, and consummates in us the new man until we attain the plenitude destined for us by the divine wisdom. This mysterious attainment of the age of Jesus Christ in our souls is the end ordained by God and the fruit of His grace and of His divine goodness.

This fruit, as we have already said, is produced, nourished and increased by the performance of those duties which become successively present, and which are made fruitful by the same divine will.

In fulfilling these duties we are always sure of possessing the "better part" because this holy will is itself the better part, it only requires to be allowed to act and that we should abandon ourselves blindly to it with perfect confidence. It is infinitely wise, powerful and amiable to those who trust themselves unreservedly to it, who love and seek it alone, and who believe with an unshaken faith and confidence that what it arranges for each moment is best, without seeking elsewhere for more or less, and without pausing to consider the connexion of these exterior works with the plans of God. This would be the refinement of self-love.

Nothing is essential, real, or of any value unless ordained by God who arranges all things and makes them useful to the soul. Apart from this divine will all is hollow, empty, null, there is nothing but falsehood, vanity, nothingness, death. The will of God is the salvation, health and life of body and soul, no matter to what subject it is applied. One must not, therefore, scrutinize too closely the suitability of things to mind or body in order to form a judgement of their value, because this is of little importance. It is the will of God which bestows through these things, no matter what they may be, an efficacious grace by which the image of Jesus Christ is renewed in our souls. One must not lay down the law nor impose limits on this divine will since it is all-powerful.

Whatever ideas may fill the mind, whatever feelings afflict the body; even if the mind should be tormented with distractions and troubles, and the body with sickness and pain, nevertheless the divine will is ever for the present moment the life of the soul and of the body; in fact, neither the one nor the other, no matter in what condition it may be, can be sustained by any other power.

The divine influence alone can sanctify us. Without it bread may be poison, and poison a salutary remedy. Without it reading only darkens the mind; with it darkness is made light. It is everything that is good and true in all things, and in all things it unites us to God, who, being infinite in all perfections, leaves nothing to be desired by the soul that possesses Him.

SECTION VI.—*On the Use of Mental Faculties.*

The exercise of mental and other faculties is only useful when instrumental of the divine action.

The mind with all the consequences of its activity might take the foremost rank among the tools employed by God, but has to be deputed to the lowest as a dangerous slave. It might be of great service if made use of in a right manner, but is a danger if not kept in subjection. When the soul longs for outward help it is made to understand that the divine action is sufficient for it. When without reason it would disclaim this outward help, the divine action shows it that such help should be received and adapted with simplicity in obedience to the order established by God, and that we should use it as a tool, not for its own sake but as though we used it not, and when deprived of all help as though we wanted nothing.

The divine action although of infinite power can only take full possession of the soul in so far as it is void of all confidence in its own action; for this confidence, being founded on a false idea of its own capacity, excludes the divine action. This is the obstacle most likely to arrest it, being in the soul itself; for, as regards obstacles that are exterior, God can change them if He so pleases into means for making progress. All is alike to Him, equally useful, or equally useless. Without the divine action all things are as nothing, and with it the veriest nothing can be turned to account.

Whether it be meditation, contemplation, vocal prayer, interior silence, or the active use of any of the faculties, either sensible and distinct, or almost imperceptible; quiet retreat, or active employment, whatever it may be in itself, even if very desirable, that which God wills for the present moment is best and all else must be regarded by the soul as being nothing at all. Thus, beholding God in all things it must take or leave them all as He pleases, and neither desire to live, nor to improve, nor to hope, except as He ordains, and never by the help of things which have neither power nor virtue except from Him. It ought, at every moment and on all occasions, to say with St. Paul, "Lord, what wilt thou have me to do?" (Acts ix, 6) without choosing this thing or that, but "whatsoever You will. The mind prefers one thing, the body another, but, Lord, I desire nothing but to accomplish Your holy will. Work, contemplation or prayer whether vocal or mental, active or passive; the prayer of faith or of understanding; that which is distinguished in kind, or gifted with universal grace: it is all nothing Lord unless made real and useful by Your will. It is to Your holy will that I devote myself and not to any of these things, however high and sublime they may be, because it is the perfection of the heart for which grace is given, and not for that of the mind."

The presence of God which sanctifies our souls is the dwelling of the Holy Trinity in the depths of our hearts when they submit to His holy will. The act of the presence of God made in contemplation effects this intimate union only like other acts that are according to the order of God.

There is, therefore, nothing unlawful in the love and esteem we have for contemplation and other pious exercises, if this love and esteem are directed entirely to the God of all goodness who willingly makes use of these means to unite our souls to Himself.

In entertaining the suite of a prince, one entertains the prince himself, and he would consider any discourtesy shown to his officers under pretence of wishing for him alone as an insult to himself.

SECTION VII.—*On the Attainment of Peace.*

There is no solid peace except in submission to the divine action.

The soul that does not attach itself solely to the will of God will find neither satisfaction nor sanctification in any other means however excellent by which it may attempt to gain them. If that which God Himself chooses for you does not content you, from whom do you expect to obtain what you desire? If you are disgusted with the meat prepared for you by the divine will itself, what food would not be insipid to so depraved a taste? No soul can be really nourished, fortified, purified, enriched, and sanctified except in fulfilling the duties of the present moment. What more would you have? As in this you can find all good, why seek it elsewhere? Do you know better than God? As he ordains it thus why do you desire it differently? Can His wisdom and goodness be deceived? When you find something to be in accordance with this divine wisdom and goodness ought you not to conclude that it must needs be excellent? Do you imagine you will find peace in resisting the Almighty? Is it not, on the contrary, this resistance which we too often continue without owning it even to ourselves which is the cause of all our troubles? It is only just, therefore, that the soul that is dissatisfied with the divine action for each present moment should be punished by being unable to find happiness in anything else. If books, the example of the saints, and spiritual conversations deprive the soul of peace; if they fill the mind without satisfying it; it is a sign that one has strayed from the path of pure abandonment to the divine action, and that one is only seeking to please oneself. To be employed in this way is to prevent God from finding an entrance. All this must be got rid of because of being an obstacle to grace. But if the divine will ordains the use of these things the soul may receive them like the rest—that is to say—as the means ordained by God which it accepts simply to use, and leaves afterwards when their moment has passed for the duties of the moment that follows. There is, in fact, nothing really good that does not emanate from the ordinance of God, and nothing, however good in itself, can be better adapted for the sanctification of the soul and the attainment of peace.

SECTION VIII.—*To Estimate Degrees of Excellence.*

The perfection of souls, and the degree of excellence to which they have attained can be gauged by their fidelity to the order established by God.

The will of God gives to all things a supernatural and divine value for the soul submitting to it. The duties it imposes, and those it contains, with all the matters over which it is diffused, become holy and perfect, because, being unlimited in power, everything it touches shares its divine character. But in order not to stray either to the right or to the left the soul should only attend to those inspirations which it believes it has received from God, by the fact that these inspirations do not withdraw it from the duties of its state. These duties are the most clear manifestation of the will of God, and nothing should take their place; in them there is nothing to fear, nothing to exclude, nor anything to be chosen. The time occupied in the fulfilment of these duties is very precious and very salutary for the soul by the indubitable fact that it is spent in accomplishing this holy will. The entire virtue of all that is called holy is in its approximation to this order established by God; therefore nothing should be rejected, nothing sought after, but everything accepted that is ordained and nothing attempted contrary to the will of God.

Books and wise counsels, vocal prayer and interior affections if they are in accordance with the will of God are instructive, and all help to guide and to unify. In contemning all sensible means to this end quietism is greatly to blame, for there are souls that are intended by God to keep always to this way. Their state of life and their attraction show this clearly enough. It is vain to picture any kind of abandonment from which all personal activity is excluded. When God requires action, sanctity is to be found in activity. Besides the duties imposed on everyone by their state of life God may require certain actions which are not included in these duties, although they may not be in any way opposed to them. An attraction and inspiration are then the signs of the divine approval. Souls conducted by God in this way will find a greater perfection in adding the things inspired to those that are commanded, taking the necessary precautions required in such cases, that the duties of their state may not clash with those things arranged by Providence.

God makes saints as He pleases, but they are made always according to His plan, and in submission to His will. This submission is true and most perfect abandonment.

Duties imposed by the state of life and by divine Providence are common to all the saints and are what God arranges for all in general. They live hidden from the world which is so evil that they are obliged to avoid its dangers: but it is not on this account that they are saints, but only on account of their submission to the will of God. The more absolute this submission becomes the higher becomes their sanctity. We must not imagine that those whose virtue is shown in wonderful and singular ways, and by unquestionable attractions and inspirations, advance less on that account in the way of abandonment. From the moment that these acts become duties by the will of God, then to be content only to fulfil the duties of a state of life, or the ordinary inspirations of Providence would be to resist God, whose holy will would no longer retain the mastery of the passing moments, and to cease practising the virtue of abandonment. Our duties must be so arranged as to be commensurate with the designs of God, and to follow the path designated by our attraction. To carry out our inspirations will then become a duty to which we must be faithful. As there are souls whose whole duty is defined by exterior laws, and who should not go beyond them because restricted by the will of God; so also there are others who, besides exterior duties, are obliged to carry out faithfully that interior rule imprinted on their hearts. It would be a foolish and frivolous curiosity to try to discover which is the most holy. Each has to follow the appointed path. Perfection consists in submitting unreservedly to the designs of God, and in fulfilling the duties of one's state in the most perfect manner possible. To compare the different states as they are in themselves can do nothing to improve us since it is neither in the amount of work, nor in the sort of duties given to us that perfection is to be found. If self-love is the motive power of our acts, or if it be not immediately crushed when discovered, our supposed abundance will be in truth absolute poverty because it is not supplied by obedience to the will of God. However, to decide the question in some way, I think that holiness can be measured by the love one has for God, and the desire to please Him, and that the more His will is the guiding principle, and His plans conformed to and loved, the greater will be the holiness, no matter what may be the means made use of. It is this that we notice in Jesus, Mary and Joseph. In their separate lives there is more of love than of greatness, and more of the spirit than of the matter. It is not written that they sought holiness in things themselves, but only in the motive with which they used them. It must therefore be concluded that one way is not more perfect than another, but that the most perfect is that which is most closely in conformity with the order established by God, whether by the accomplishment of exterior duties, or by interior dispositions.

SECTION IX.—*Sanctity Made Easy.*

Conclusion of the first chapter. How easy sanctity becomes when this doctrine is properly understood.

I believe that if those souls that tend towards sanctity were instructed as to the conduct they ought to follow, they would be spared a good deal of trouble. I speak as much of people in the world as of others. If they could realise the merit concealed in the actions of each moment of the day: I mean in each of the daily duties of their state of life, and if they could be persuaded that sanctity is founded on that to which they give no heed as being altogether irrelevant, they would indeed be happy. If, besides, they understood that to attain the utmost height of perfection, the safest and surest way is to accept the crosses sent them by Providence at every moment, that the true philosopher's stone is submission to the will of God which changes into divine gold all their occupations, troubles, and sufferings, what consolation would be theirs! What courage would they not derive from the thought that to acquire the friendship of God, and to arrive at eternal glory, they had but to do what they were doing, but to suffer what they were suffering, and that what they wasted and counted as nothing would suffice to enable them to arrive at eminent sanctity: far more so than extraordinary states and wonderful works. O my God! how much I long to be the missionary of Your holy will, and to teach all men that there is nothing more easy, more attainable, more within reach, and in the power of everyone, than sanctity. How I wish that I could make them understand that just as the good and the bad thief had the same things to do and to suffer; so also two persons, one of whom is worldly and the other leading an interior and wholly spiritual life have, neither of them, anything different to do or to suffer; but that one is sanctified and attains eternal happiness by submission to Your holy will in those very things by which the other is damned because he does them to please himself, or endures them with reluctance and rebellion. This proves that it is only the heart that is different. Oh! all you that read this, it will cost you no more than to do what you are doing, to suffer what you are suffering, only act and suffer in a holy manner. It is the heart that must be changed. When I say heart, I mean will. Sanctity, then, consists in willing all that God wills for us. Yes! sanctity of heart is a simple "fiat," a conformity of will with the will of God.

What could be more easy, and who could refuse to love a will so kind and so good? Let us love it then, and this love alone will make everything in us divine.

CHAPTER II.

THE DIVINE ACTION WORKS UNCEASINGLY
FOR THE SANCTIFICATION OF SOULS.

SECTION I.—*The Unceasing Work of God.*

The divine action, although only visible to the eye of faith, is everywhere, and always present.

All creatures that exist are in the hands of God. The action of the creature can only be perceived by the senses, but faith sees in all things the action of the Creator. It believes that in Jesus Christ all things live, and that His divine operation continues to the end of time, embracing the passing moment and the smallest created atom in its hidden life and mysterious action. The action of the creature is a veil which covers the profound mysteries of the divine operation. After the Resurrection Jesus Christ took His disciples by surprise in His various apparitions. He showed Himself to them under various disguises and, in the act of making Himself known to them, disappeared. This same Jesus, ever living, ever working, still takes by surprise those souls whose faith is weak and wavering.

There is not a moment in which God does not present Himself under the cover of some pain to be endured, of some consolation to be enjoyed, or of some duty to be performed. All that takes place within us, around us, or through us, contains and conceals His divine action.

It is really and truly there present, but invisibly present, so that we are always surprised and do not recognise His operation until it has ceased. If we could lift the veil, and if we were attentive and watchful God would continually reveal Himself to us, and we should see His divine action in everything that happened to us, and rejoice in it. At each successive occurrence we should exclaim: "It is the Lord," and we should accept every fresh circumstance as a gift of God. We should look upon creatures as feeble tools in the hands of an able workman, and should discover easily that nothing was wanting to us, and that the constant providence of God disposed Him to bestow upon us at every moment whatever we required. If only we had faith we should show good-will to all creatures; we should cherish them and be interiorly grateful to them as serving, by God's will, for our perfection. If we lived the life of faith without intermission we should have an uninterrupted commerce with God and a constant familiar intercourse with Him. What the air is for the transmission of our thoughts and words, such would be our actions and sufferings for those of God. They would be as the substance of His words, and in all external events we should see nothing but what was excellent and holy. This union is effected on earth by faith, in Heaven by glory; the only difference is in the method of its working. God is interpreted by faith. Without the light of faith creation would speak to us in vain. It is a writing in cypher in which we find nothing but confusion, and entangled mesh from which no one would expect to hear the voice of God. But as Moses saw the fire of divine charity in the burning bush, so faith gives us the clue to the cypher, and reveals to us, in this mass of confusion, marvels of divine wisdom. Faith changes the face of the earth; by it the heart is raised, entranced and becomes conversant with heavenly things. Faith is our light in this life. By it we possess the truth without seeing it; we touch what we cannot feel, and see what is not evident to the senses. By it we view the world as though it did not exist. It is the key of the treasure house, the key of the abyss of the science of God. It is faith that teaches us the hollowness of created things; By it God reveals and manifests Himself in all things. By faith the veil is torn aside to reveal the eternal truth.

All that we see is nothing but vanity and deceit; truth can be found only in God. What a difference between the thoughts of God and the illusions of man! How is it that although continually warned that everything that happens in the world is but a shadow, a figure, a mystery of faith, we look at the outside only and do not perceive the enigma they contain?

We fall into this trap like men without sense instead of raising our eyes to the principle, source and origin of all things, in which they all have their right name and just proportions, in which everything is supernatural, divine, and sanctifying; in which all is part of the plenitude of Jesus Christ, and each circumstance is as a stone towards the construction of the heavenly Jerusalem, and all helps to build a dwelling for us in that marvellous city.

We live according to what we see and feel and wander like madmen in a labyrinth of darkness and illusion for want of the light of faith which would guide us safely through it. By means of faith we should be able to aspire after God and to live for Him alone, forsaking and going beyond mere figures.

SECTION II.—*By Faith the Operation of God is recognised.*

The more hidden the divine operation beneath an outwardly repulsive appearance, the more visible it is to the eye of faith.

The soul, enlightened by faith, judges of things in a very different way to those who, having only the standard of the senses by which to measure them, ignore the inestimable treasure they contain. He who knows that a certain person in disguise is the king, behaves towards him very differently to another who, only perceiving an ordinary man, treats him accordingly. In the same way the soul that recognises the will of God in every smallest event, and also in those that are most distressing and direful, receives all with an equal joy, pleasure and respect. It throws open all its doors to receive with honour what others fear and fly from with horror. The outward appearance may be mean and contemptible, but beneath this abject garb the heart discovers and honours the majesty of the king. The deeper the abasement of his entry in such a guise and in secret the more does the heart become filled with love. I cannot describe what the heart feels when it accepts the divine will in such humble, poor, and mean disguises. Ah! how the sight of God, poor and humble, lodged in a stable, lying on straw, weeping and trembling, pierced the loving heart of Mary! Ask the inhabitants of Bethlehem what they thought of the Child. You know what answer they gave, and how they would have paid court to Him had He been lodged in a palace surrounded by the state due to princes. Then ask Mary and Joseph, the Magi and the Shepherds. They will tell you that they found in this extreme poverty an indescribable tenderness, and an infinite dignity worthy of the majesty of God. Faith is strengthened, increased and enriched by those things that escape the senses; the less there is to see, the more there is to believe. To adore Jesus on Thabor, to accept the will of God in extraordinary circumstances does not indicate a life animated by such great faith as to love the will of God in ordinary things and to adore Jesus on the Cross; for faith cannot be said to be real, living faith until it is tried, and has triumphed over every effort for its destruction. War with the senses enables faith to obtain a more glorious victory. To consider God equally good in things that are petty and ordinary as in those that are great and uncommon is to have a faith that is not ordinary, but great and extraordinary.

To be satisfied with the present moment is to delight in, and to adore the divine will in all that has to be done or suffered in all that succession of events that fill, as they pass, each present moment. Those souls that have this disposition adore God with redoubled love and respect in each consecutive humiliating condition; nothing can hide Him from the piercing eye of faith. The louder the senses proclaim that in this, or that, there is no God; the more firmly do these souls clasp and embrace their "bundle of myrrh." Nothing daunts them, nothing disgusts them.

Mary, when the apostles fled, remained steadfast at the foot of the Cross. She owned Jesus as her Son when He was disfigured with wounds, and covered with mud and spittle. The wounds that disfigured Him made Him only more lovable and adorable in the eyes of this tender Mother. The more awful were the blasphemies uttered against Him, so much the deeper became her veneration and respect.

The life of faith is nothing less than the continued pursuit of

God through all that disguises, disfigures, destroys and, so to say, annihilates Him. It is in very truth a reproduction of the life of Mary who, from the Stable to the Cross, remained unalterably united to that God whom all the world misunderstood, abandoned, and persecuted. In like manner faithful souls endure a constant succession of trials. God hides beneath veils of darkness and illusive appearances which make His will difficult to recognise; but in spite of every obstacle these souls follow Him and love Him even to the death of the Cross. They know that, leaving the darkness they must run after the light of this divine Sun which, from its rising to its setting, however dark and thick may be the clouds that obscure it, enlightens, warms, and inflames the faithful hearts that bless, praise and contemplate it during the whole circle of its mysterious course.

Pursue then without ceasing, ye faithful souls, this beloved Spouse who with giant strides passes from one extremity of the heavens to the other. If you be content and untiring nothing will have power to hide Him from you. He moves above the smallest blades of grass as above the mighty cedar. The grains of sand are under His feet as well as the huge mountains. Wherever you may turn, there you will find His footprints, and in following them perseveringly you will find Him wherever you may be.

Oh! what delightful peace we enjoy when we have learnt by faith to find God thus in all His creatures! Then is darkness luminous, and bitterness sweet. Faith, while showing us things as they are, changes their ugliness into beauty, and their malice into virtue. Faith is the mother of sweetness, confidence and joy. It cannot help feeling tenderness and compassion for its enemies by whose means it is so immeasurably enriched. The greater the harshness and severity of the creature, the greater by the operation of God, is the advantage to the soul. While the human instrument strives to do harm, the divine Workman in whose hands it is, makes use of its very malice to remove from the soul all that might be prejudicial to it.

The will of God has nothing but sweetness, favours and treasures for submissive souls; it is impossible to repose too much confidence in it, nor to abandon oneself to it too utterly. It always acts for, and desires that which is most conducive to our perfection, provided we allow it to act. Faith does not doubt. The more unfaithful, uncertain, and rebellious are the senses, the louder faith cries: "all is well, it is the will of God." There is nothing that the eye of faith does not penetrate, nothing that the power of faith does not overcome. It passes through the thick darkness, and, no matter what clouds may gather, it goes straight to the truth, and holding to it firmly will never let it go.

SECTION III.—*How to Discover what is the Will of God.*

The divine action places before us at every moment things of infinite value, and gives them to us according to the measure of our faith and love.

If we understood how to see in each moment some manifestation of the will of God we should find therein also all that our hearts could desire. In fact there could be nothing more reasonable, more perfect, more divine than the will of God. Could any change of time, place, or circumstance alter or increase its infinite value? If you possess the secret of discovering it at every moment and in everything, then you possess all that is most precious, and most worthy to be desired. What is it that you desire, you who aim at perfection? Give yourselves full scope. Your wishes need have no measure, no limit. However much you may desire I can show you how to attain it, even though it be infinite. There is never a moment in which I cannot enable you to obtain all that you can desire. The present is ever filled with infinite treasure, it contains more than you have capacity to hold. Faith is the measure. Believe, and it will be done to you accordingly. Love also is the measure. The more the heart loves, the more it desires; and the more it desires, so much the more will it receive. The will of God is at each moment before us like an immense, inexhaustible ocean that no human heart can fathom; but none can receive from it more than he has capacity to contain, it is necessary to enlarge this capacity by faith, confidence, and love.

The whole creation cannot fill the human heart, for it is greater than all that is not God. It is on a higher plane than the

the place of light, ignorance of knowledge, and one neither sees nor understands. The sacred Scripture is the mysterious utterance of a God yet more mysterious; and the events of the world are the obscure language of this same hidden and unknown God. They are mere drops from an ocean of midnight darkness, and partake of the nature of their source. The fall of the angels and of Adam; the impiety and idolatry of men before and after the Deluge up to the time of the Patriarchs who knew, and related to their children the history of the Creation, and of the still recent preservation from the universal deluge; these are, indeed, very obscure words of holy Scripture. That, at the coming of the Messiah, only a handful of men should be preserved from idolatry in the general ruin and overthrow of faith throughout the world: that impiety should prove always dominant, always powerful, and the small numbers of the upholders of truth should be ever persecuted and maltreated, seems incredible! Consider the treatment of Jesus Christ. Think of the plagues of the Apocalypse, yet these are words of God. They are what He has revealed! He has dictated them! And the effect of these terrible mysteries which will continue till the end of time is still the living word, teaching us His wisdom, power, and goodness. All the events which form the world's history show forth these divine attributes; all teach the same adorable word. We cannot doubt it, although we do not see. What is meant by the existence of Turks, heretics, and all the other enemies of the Church? Surely they all proclaim loudly the divine perfections. Pharaoh and the impious men who follow his example are allowed to exist only for that purpose, but assuredly, unless beheld with the eye of faith, it would all have the exactly contrary appearance. To behold divine mysteries it is necessary to shut the eyes to what is external, and to cease to reason. You speak, Lord, to the generality of men by great public events. Every resolution is as a wave from the sea of Your providence, raising storms and tempests in the minds of those who question Your mysterious action. You speak also to each individual soul by the circumstances occurring at every moment of life. Instead, however, of hearing Your voice in these events, and receiving with awe what is obscure and mysterious in these Your words,

men see in them only the outward aspect, or chance, or the
caprice of others, and censure everything. They would like to
add, or diminish, or reform, and to allow themselves absolute
liberty to commit any excess, the least of which would be a
criminal and unheard-of outrage. They respect the holy
Scriptures, however, and will not permit the addition of even a
single comma. "It is the word of God" say they, "and is altogether holy and true. If we cannot understand it, it is all the
more wonderful and we must give glory to God, and render
justice to the depths of His wisdom." All this is perfectly true,
but when you read God's word from moment to moment, not
written with ink on paper, but on your soul with suffering, and
the daily actions that you have to perform, does it not merit
some attention on your part? How is it that you cannot see the
will of God in all this? Instead you find fault with everything that
happens, nothing pleases you. Do you not see that you are gaug-
ing everything by the senses, and by reason, not by faith the only
true standard; and that when you read the word of God in the
sacred Scriptures with the eye of faith, you do wrong to make
use only of your reason in reading the word in His marvellous
operations.

SECTION V.—*The action of Jesus Christ in the Souls of Men.*

The divine action continues to write in the hearts of men the
work begun by the holy Scriptures, but the characters made use
of in this writing will not be visible till the day of judgment.

"Jesus Christ yesterday, to-day, and for ever" (Heb. xiii, 8),
says the Apostle. From the beginning of the world He was, as
God, the first cause of the existence of souls. He has partici-
pated as man from the first instant of His incarnation, in this
prerogative of His divinity. During the whole course of our life
He acts within our souls. The time that will elapse till the end of
the world is but as a day; and this day abounds with His action.
Jesus Christ has lived and lives still. He began from Himself and
will continue in His Saints a life that will never end. O life of
Jesus! comprehending and extending beyond all the centuries of

time, life effecting new operations of grace at every moment; if no one is capable of understanding all that could be written of the actual life of Jesus, all that He did and said while He was on earth; if the Gospel merely outlines a few of its features; how many Gospels would have to be written to record the history of all the moments of this mystical life of Jesus Christ in which miracles are multiplied to infinity and eternity. If the beginning of His natural life is so hidden yet so fruitful, what can be said of the divine action of that life of which every age of the world is the history?

The Holy Spirit has pointed out in infallible and incontestable characters, some moments in that ocean of time, in the Sacred Scriptures. In them we see by what secret and mysterious ways He has brought Jesus before the world. Amidst the confusion of the races of men can be distinguished the origin, race, and genealogy of this, the first-born. The whole of the Old Testament is but an outline of the profound mystery of this divine work; it contains only what is necessary to relate concerning the advent of Jesus Christ. The Holy Spirit has kept all the rest hidden among the treasures of His wisdom. From this ocean of the divine activity He only allows a tiny stream to escape, and this stream having gained its way to Jesus is lost in the Apostles, and has been engulfed in the Apocalypse; so that the history of this divine activity consisting of the life of Jesus in the souls of the just to the end of time, can only be divined by faith. As the truth of God has been made known by word of mouth, so His charity is manifested by action. The Holy Spirit continues to carry on the work of our Saviour. While helping the Church to preach the Gospel of Jesus Christ, He writes His own Gospel in the hearts of the just. All their actions, every moment of their lives, are the Gospel of the Holy Spirit. The souls of the saints are the paper, the sufferings and actions the ink. The Holy Spirit with the pen of His power writes a living Gospel, but a Gospel that cannot be read until it has left the press of this life, and has been published on the day of eternity. Oh! great history! grand book written by the Holy Spirit in this present time! It is still in the press. There is never a day when the type is not arranged, when the ink is not applied, or the pages are not printed. We are still in the dark night of faith. The paper is blacker than the ink, and there is great confusion in the type. It is written in characters of another world and there is no understanding it except in Heaven. If we could see the life of God, and behold all creatures, not as they are in themselves, but as they exist in their first cause; and if again we could see the life of God in all His creatures, and could understand how the divine action animates them, and impels them all to press forward by different ways to the same goal, we should realize that all has a meaning, a measure, a connexion in this divine work. But how can we read a book the characters of which are foreign to us, the letters innumerable, the type reversed, and the pages blotted with ink? If the transposition of twenty-five letters is incomprehensible as sufficing for the composition of a well-nigh infinite number of different volumes, each admirable of its kind, who can explain the works of God in the universe? Who can read and understand the meaning of so vast a book in which there is no letter but has its particular character, and encloses in its apparent insignificance the most profound mysteries? Mysteries can neither be seen nor felt, they are objects of faith. Faith judges of their virtue and truth only by their origin, for they are so obscure in themselves that all that they show only serves to hide them and to blind those who judge only by reason.

"Teach me, divine Spirit, to read in this book of life. I desire to become Your disciple and, like a little child, to believe what I cannot understand, and cannot see. Sufficient for me that it is my Master who speaks. He says that! He pronounces this! He arranges the letters in such a fashion! He makes Himself heard in such a manner! That is enough. I decide that all is exactly as He says. I do not see the reason, but He is the infallible truth, therefore all that He says, all that He does is true. He groups His letters to form a word, and different letters again to form another word. There may be three only, or six; then no more are necessary, and fewer would destroy the sense. He who reads the thoughts of men is the only one who can bring these letters together, and write the words. All has meaning, all has perfect sense. This line ends here because He makes it do so. Not a comma is missing, and there is no unnecessary full-stop. At present I believe, but in the glory to come when so many mysteries will be revealed, I shall see plainly what now I so little understand.

Then what appears to me at present so intricate, so perplexing, so foolish, so inconsistent, so imaginary, will all be entrancing and will delight me eternally by the beauty, order, knowledge, wisdom, and the incomprehensible wonders it will all display."

SECTION VI.—*The Treatment of the Divine Action.*

The divine action as manifested in daily events is treated by many Christians in as unworthy a manner as the Jews treated the Sacred Body of Jesus.

The world is full of infidelity. How unworthy are its thoughts of God! It complains continually of the divine action in a way that it would not dare to use towards the lowest workman about his trade. It would reduce God to act only within the limits, and following the rules of its feeble reason. It presumes to imagine it can improve upon His acts. These are nothing but complaints and murmurings. We are surprised at the treatment endured by Jesus Christ at the hands of the Jews, but, O divine love! adorable will! infallible truth! in what way are you treated? Can the divine will ever be inopportune? Can it be mistaken? "But there is this business of mine! I require such a thing! The necessary helps have been taken from me. That man thwarts all my good works, is it not most unreasonable? This illness comes on just when my health is most necessary to me." To all this there is but one answer—that the will of God is the only thing necessary, therefore what it does not grant must be useless. My good souls! nothing is wanting to you. If you only knew what these events really are that you call misfortunes, accidents, and disappointments, and in which you can see nothing but what is irrelevant, or unreasonable, you would be deeply ashamed and excuse yourselves of your complainings as of blasphemies; but you never think of them as being the will of God, and His adorable will is blasphemed by His own children who refuse to acknowledge it. When You were on earth, O my Jesus, the Jews treated You as a demonaic, and called You a Samaritan; and now, although it is acknowledged that You live and work through all the centuries of time, how is Your adorable will received? that will worthy of all benediction and praise for ever. Has one moment passed from the creation to the present time, and will one moment pass even to the day of judgment in which the holy name of God will not deserve praise; that name which fills all the ages, and everything which takes place in the ages, that name by which everything is sanctified? What! can the will of God do me harm? Shall I fear, or fly from the will of God? And where shall I find anything better if I dread the divine action in my regard, or regret the effect of His divine will? We ought to listen attentively to the words uttered in the depths of our heart at every moment. If our sense and reason do not understand nor enter into the truth and goodness of these words, is it not because they are incapable of appreciating divine truths? Ought I to wonder that my reason is bewildered by mysteries? When God speaks it is a mystery, and therefore a death-blow to my senses and reason, for it is the nature of mysteries to compel the sacrifice of both. Mystery makes the soul live by faith; for all the rest there is nothing but contradiction. The divine action by one and the same stroke kills and gives life; the more one feels the death to the senses and reason, the more convinced should one become that it gives life to the soul. The more obscure the mystery to us, the more light it contains in itself. This is why a simple soul will discover a more divine meaning in that which has the least appearance of having any.

The life of faith is a continual struggle against the senses.

SECTION VII.—*The Hidden Work of Divine Love.*

The divine love is communicated to us through every creature under veils, like the Eucharistic species.

What great truths are hidden even from Christians who imagine themselves most enlightened! How many are there amongst them who understand that every cross, every action, every attraction according to the designs of God, give God to us in a way that nothing can better explain than a comparison with the most august mystery? Nevertheless there is nothing more certain. Does not reason as well as faith reveal to us the real presence of divine love in all creatures, and in all the events of life, as indubitably as the words of Jesus Christ and of the Church reveal the real presence of the sacred flesh of our Saviour under the Eucharistic species? Do we not know that by all creatures, and by every event the divine love desires to unite us to Himself, that He has ordained, arranged, or permitted everything about us, everything that happens to us with a view to this union? This is the ultimate object of all His designs to attain which He makes use of the worst of His creatures as well as of the best, and of the most distressing events as well as of those which are pleasant and agreeable. Our communion with Him is even more meritorious when the means that serve to make it closer are repugnant to nature. If this be true, every moment of our lives may be a kind of communion with the divine love, and this communion of every moment may produce as much fruit in our souls as that which we receive in the Communion of the Body and Blood of the Son of God. This latter, it is true, is efficacious sacramentally which the former cannot be, but on the other hand, how much more frequently can it not be renewed, and what great increase of merit it can acquire by the more perfect dispositions with which it may be accomplished. Consequently how true it is that the more holy the life the more mysterious it becomes by its apparent simplicity and littleness. O great feast! O perpetual festival! God! given and received under all that is most feeble, foolish and worthless upon earth! God chooses that which nature abhors, and human prudence rejects. Of these He makes mysteries, sacraments of love, and by that which seems as if it would do most harm to souls, He gives Himself to them as often and as much as they desire to possess Him.

SECTION VIII.—*Experimental Science.*

That which is sent us at the present moment is the most useful because it is intended especially for us.

We can only be well instructed by the words which God utters expressly for us. No one becomes learned in the science of God either by the reading of books, or by the inquisitive investigation of history. The science that is acquired by such means is vain and confused, producing much pride. That which instructs us is what happens from one moment to another producing in us that experimental science which Jesus Christ Himself willed to acquire before instructing others. In fact this was the only science in which He could grow, according to the expression of the holy Gospel; because being God there was no degree of speculative science which He did not possess. Therefore if this experimental science was useful to the Word incarnate Himself, to us it is absolutely necessary if we wish to touch the hearts of those whom God sends to us. It is impossible perfectly to understand anything that experience has not taught us by suffering or by action. This is the school of the Holy Spirit who in this way speaks life-giving words to the soul, and those which He speaks to us through others come from the same source.

Reading and seeing become fruitful and possess virtue and light only by the acquisition of this divine science, otherwise they are like dough to which leaven is necessary, and the salt of experience to season it. And since without this salt, we have only vague ideas to act upon, we are like visionaries, who, though knowing the roads that lead to all the towns, yet lose their way going to their own house.

We must listen to God from moment to moment to become learned in the theology of virtue which is entirely practical and experimental. Do not attend therefore to what is said to others, but listen to that which is said to you and for you; there will be enough to exercise your faith because this interior language of God exercises, purifies, and increases it by its very obscurity.

SECTION IX.—*The Will of God in the Present Moment is the Source of Sanctity.*

O, all you who thirst, learn that you have not far to go to find the fountain of living waters; it flows quite close to you in the present moment; therefore hasten to find it. Why, with the fountain so near, do you tire yourselves with running about after every little rill? These only increase your thirst by giving only a few drops, whereas the source is inexhaustible. If you desire to think, to write, and to speak like the Prophets, the Apostles, and the Saints, you must give yourself up, as they did, to the inspirations of God. O unknown Love! it seems as if Your wonders were finished and nothing remained but to copy Your ancient works, and to quote Your past discourses! And no one sees that Your inexhaustible activity is a source of new thoughts, of fresh sufferings and further actions: of new Patriarchs, Apostles, Prophets, and Saints who have no need to copy the lives and writings of the others, but only to live in perpetual abandonment to Your secret operations. We hear of nothing on all sides but "the first centuries," "the time of the Saints." What a strange way of talking! Is not all time a succession of the effects of the divine operation, working at every instant, filling, sanctifying, and supernaturalising them all? Has there ever been an ancient method of abandonment to this operation which is now out of season? Had the Saints of the first ages any other secret than that of becoming from moment to moment whatever the divine power willed to make them? And will this power cease to pour forth its glory on the souls which abandon themselves to it without reserve.

O Love eternal, adorable, ever fruitful, and ever marvellous! May the divine operation of my God be my book, my doctrine, my science. In it are my thoughts, my words, my actions, and my sufferings. Not by consulting Your former works shall I become what You would have me to be; but by receiving You in everything. By that ancient road, the only royal road, the road of our fathers shall I be enlightened, and shall speak as they spoke. It is thus that I would imitate them all, quote them all, copy them all.

SECTION X.—*God Makes Known His Will Through Creatures.*

In the present moment are made manifest the name of God, and the coming of His Kingdom.

The present moment is the ambassador of God to declare His mandates. The heart listens and pronounces its "fiat." Thus the soul advances by all these things and flows out from its centre to its goal. It never stops but sails with every wind. Any and every direction leads equally to the shore of infinity. Everything is a help to it, and is, without exception, an instrument of sanctity. The one thing necessary can always be found for it in the present moment. It is no longer a choice between prayer and silence, seclusion and society, reading and writing, meditation and cessation of thought, flight from and seeking after spiritual consolations, abundance and dearth, feebleness and health, life and death, but it is all that each moment presents by the will of God. In this is despoilment, abnegation, renunciation of all things created, either in reality or affectively, in order to retain nothing of self, or for self, to be in all things submissive to the will of God and to please Him; making it our sole satisfaction to sustain the present moment as though there were nothing else to hope for in the world.

If all that happens to a soul abandoned to God is all that is necessary for it, then we can understand that nothing can be wanting to it, and that it should never pity itself, for this would be a want of faith and living according to reason and the senses which are never satisfied, as they cannot perceive the sufficiency of grace possessed by the soul. To hallow the name of God, is according to the meaning of the holy Scripture, to recognise His sanctity in all things and to love and adore Him in them. Things, in fact, proceed from the mouth of God like words. That which God does at each moment is a divine thought expressed by a created thing, therefore all those things by which He intimates His will to us are so many names and words by which He makes known His wishes. His will is unity and has but one name, unknown, and ineffable; but it is infinitely diverse in its effects, which are, as it were, so many different characters which it assumes. To hallow the Name of God is to know, to adore, and to love the ineffable Being whom this name designates. It is also to know, to adore and to love His adorable will at every moment and in all its decrees, regarding them all as so many veils, shadows and names of this holy and everlasting will.

It is holy in all its works, holy in all its words, holy in all its diverse characters, holy in all the names it bears.

It was for this reason that Job blessed the name of God in his utter desolation. Instead of looking upon his condition as ruin, he called it the name of God and by blessing it he protested that the divine will under whatever name or form it might appear, even though expressed by the most terrible catastrophes, was holy. David also blessed it at all times, and in all places. It is then, by this continual recognition of the will of God as manifested and revealed in all things, that He reigns in us, that His will is done on earth as it is in Heaven, and that our souls obtain nourishment. The whole matter of that incomparable prayer prescribed by Jesus Christ is comprised and contained in abandonment to the divine will. Many times daily it is recited vocally by the command of God and of Holy Church, but we repeat it at every moment in the centre of our hearts when we love to do, or to suffer whatever this holy will ordains. That which takes time to repeat in words, the heart pronounces at every moment, and it is in this way that simple-minded souls are called to bless God. Nevertheless they cannot bless Him as much as they desire, and this inability is a subject of grief to them; so true is it that by the very means that seem like privations, God bestows graces and favours on faithful souls. To enrich the soul at the expense of the senses, filling it by so much the more as they experience the more terrible emptiness, is a secret of the divine wisdom.

The events of every moment bear the impress of the will of God, and of His adorable Name. How holy is this name! It is right, therefore, to bless it, to treat it as a kind of sacrament which by its own virtue sanctifies those souls which place no obstacles in its way.

Everything bearing the impress of this august Name should be held in the most profound veneration. It is a divine manna from Heaven, and imparts a constant increase of grace. It is the reign of holiness in the soul, the bread of angels eaten on earth as well as in Heaven. We can no longer consider our moments as trifles since in them is a whole kingdom of sanctity and food for angels.

"Yes, Lord, may your kingdom come in my heart to sanctify it, to nourish it, to purify it, and to render it victorious over all its enemies. Moment most precious! How insignificant in the eyes of the vulgar, but how great in those enlightened by faith. If it is great also in the eyes of my Father who is in Heaven, how can I regard it as insignificant? All that comes from His hand is essentially good and bears the impress of its origin."

SECTION XI.—*Everything is Supernaturalised by the Divine Action.*

The divine action incites souls to aim at the most eminent sanctity; all that is required on the part of the soul is abandonment to this action.

It is only from want of knowing how to make use of the divine action that so many Christians pass their lives in anxiously pursuing a multitude of methods which might prove useful if ordained by this divine action, but which by preventing a simple union with it, become positively harmful. All this multiplicity fails to impart that which can only be found in the principle of all life, that which is continually present with us, and which stamps each of its tools with a character of its own and makes it work with an incomparable fitness. Jesus is sent to us as a Master to whom we do not sufficiently attend. He speaks to every heart, and to each He utters the word of life, the only word applicable to us, but we do not hear it. We want to know what He has said to others and do not listen when He speaks to ourselves. We do not sufficiently regard things as having been supernaturalised by the divine action. We should always accept them with the perfect confidence they merit; with an open mind and with generosity, and be sure that nothing will harm those who act thus. This vast activity, which is in itself ever the same from the beginning to the end of time, is employed with every moment, pouring its immensity and virtue on the souls which adore it, love it, and rejoice in it alone.

You say you would be delighted to find an opportunity of dying for God, and would be completely satisfied with some such action, or with a life leading to the same result. To lose all, to die forsaken, to sacrifice your life for others, these are indeed charming ideas! But as for me, Lord, I glorify in all things the might of Your will in which I find all the happiness of martyrdom, austerities, and good works for others. Your will is enough, and I am content to live and to die as it decrees. In itself it is more pleasing to me than all the attributes of the instruments of which it makes use, or than their effects, because it pervades all, makes all divine, and changes all into itself. It is all heavenly to me, and every one of my moments is a genuine divine action, and living or dying I shall always be satisfied with it. Yes, divine Love, I shall no longer single out times or ways, but shall welcome You always and in any fashion. It seems to me, O divine Will, as if You had revealed Your immensity to me; I will therefore take no steps save in the bosom of Your infinity, You who are the same yesterday, to-day, and for ever. The unceasing torrent of graces has its rise in You. It is from You that it flows, is carried on, and made active. Therefore it is not within the narrow limits of a book, or the life of a saint, or in some sublime idea that I ought to seek You. These are but drops of that ocean which is poured out over every creature and in which they are all immersed. They are mere atoms that disappear in this deep abyss. I will no longer seek this action in the thoughts of spiritual persons. I will no longer beg my bread from door to door, nor pay court to creatures, but I will live as the child of an infinitely good, wise, and powerful father whom I desire to please, and to make happy. I wish to live according to my faith, and since the divine action is applied by every single thing and at every moment for my perfection, I will live on this immense fortune, this certain income, and in the most profitable manner.

Is there any creature whose action can equal that of God? Why then should I go to creatures for help since all that happens to me is the work of His uncreated hand? Creatures are powerless, ignorant, and without affection and I should die of thirst rushing like this from one fountain to another, from one stream to another when there is a sea at hand, the waters of which encompass me on every side. All that happens to me therefore will be food for my nourishment, water for my cleansing, fire for my purification, and a channel of grace for all my needs. That which I might endeavour to find in other ways seeks me incessantly and gives itself to me through all creatures.

O Love of God! how is it that all creatures do not know how freely you lavish Yourself and Your favours on them while they are seeking You in byways and corners where You are not to be found? How foolish to refuse to breathe the open air! to search for a spot on which to place the foot when there is the whole countryside before you; to be unable to find water when there is a whole deluge at your service, nor to possess and enjoy God, nor to recognise His action when it is present in all things. You search for hidden ways of belonging to God, good people, but the only way is that of making use of whatever He sends you. All leads to union, to perfection, except what is sinful or not a duty. All that is necessary is to accept everything, placing no obstacle in the way of its action but letting it accomplish its work. All things are intended to guide, raise, and support you, and are in the hand of God whose action is vaster and more present than the elements of earth, air, and water. Even by means of the senses God will enter, provided they are used only as He ordains, because everything contrary to His will must be resisted. There is not a single atom that goes to form part of your being, even to the marrow of the bones, that is not formed by the divine power. From it all things proceed, by it all things are made. Your very life-blood flows through your veins by the movement this power imparts to it, and all the fluctuations that exist between strength and weakness, languor and liveliness, life and death, are divine instruments put in motion to effect your sanctification. Under its influence all bodily states become operations of grace. From this invisible hand come all your opinions, all your ideas on whatever subject they may be formed. What this action will effect in you, you will learn by successive experiences, for there is no created heart or mind that can teach it to you. Your life flows on uninterruptedly in this unsounded abyss in which each present moment contains all that is best for

you, and as such must be loved and esteemed. It is necessary to
have a perfect confidence in this action which of itself can do
nothing but what is good.

Yes, divine Love! to what heights of supernatural, sublime,
admirable and incomparable virtue would all souls arrive if they
would but be satisfied with Your action!

Yes, if they would leave the matter in this divine hand they
would attain to an eminent degree of perfection! Everyone
would arrive at it because it is offered to all. No effort is required
because the work accomplishes itself. Every soul possesses in
You an infinitely perfect model, and by your action which works
ceaselessly to this end, is rendered like this model. If all souls
were faithful copies of this divine example they would all speak,
act, and live divinely. They would not require to copy each
other, but would be singled out by the divine influence, and
each would be rendered unique by the most simple and ordinary things.

By what means, O my God, I can make your creatures appreciate what is offered to them? Must I who possess so great a
treasure with which I could enrich the whole world, see souls
perish in poverty? Must I behold them withering like plants in
a desert when I can show them the source of living waters?

Come, foolish souls, you who have not an atom of sensible
devotion, you too who possess no talent nor even the rudiments
of education, you who cannot understand a single spiritual term,
who stand astonished at the eloquence of the learned whom you
admire; come, and I will teach you a secret which will place you
far beyond these clever minds. I will make perfection so easy to
you that you will find it everywhere and in everything. I will
unite you to God, and make you walk hand in hand with Him
from the moment that you begin practising what I will teach
you. Come, not to study the map of the spiritual country, but to
possess it, to walk in it at your ease without fear of losing your
way. Come, not to study the theory of divine grace, nor to find
out what it has accomplished in the past and still continues to
accomplish; but to become simply subject to its operations. It is
not necessary that you should understand what it has said to
others, nor to repeat the words intended only for them and

which you have overheard, but you, yourself, will receive from it what is best for you.

SECTION XII.—*The Divine Word our Model.*

The divine action alone can sanctify us, for that alone can make us imitate the divine Example of our perfection.

In course of time the idea formed by the Eternal Wisdom of all things is carried out by divine action. All things have, in God, their likeness, and are recognised and known by the divine Wisdom. Should you know all those things that are not for you, such knowledge would be no guide to you in any way. The divine action beholds in the Word the idea after which you ought to be formed and this example is always before it. It sees in the Word all that is necessary for the sanctification of every soul. The holy Scriptures contain one part, and the workings of the divine action in the interior of the soul, after the example set forth by the Word, complete the work. We must understand that the only way of receiving the impression of this eternal idea is to remain quietly amenable to it; and that neither efforts, nor mental speculations can do anything to that end. It is obvious that a work such as this cannot be effected by cleverness, intelligence, nor subtlety of mind, but only by the passive way of abandonment to, its reception, and by yielding to it like metal in a mould, or canvas under the pencil, or stone in the hands of the sculptor. It is evident that to know all the divine mysteries of God is by no means the way in which by His will we are made to resemble His image, that image which the Word has formed of us; that our resemblance to the divine type can only be formed in us by the impression of the seal of the divine action, and that this impression is not produced in the mind by ideas, but in the will by abandonment. The wisdom of the just soul consists in being content with what is intended for it! in confining itself within the boundary of its path, and not trespassing beyond its limit. It is not inquisitive about God's ways of acting, but is content as regards itself with the arrangements of His will, making no effort to discover its meaning by comparisons or conjectures, but only desiring to understand what each moment reveals. It listens to the voice of the Word when it sounds in the depths of the heart, it does not inquire as to what the divine Spouse has said to others, but is satisfied with what it receives for itself, so that moment by moment it becomes, in this way, divinised without its knowledge. It is thus that the divine Word converses with His spouse, by the solid effects of His action which the spouse without scrutinising curiously, accepts with loving gratitude. Thus the spirituality of such a soul is perfectly simple, absolutely solid, and thoroughly diffused throughout its entire being. Its actions are not determined by ideas nor by a confusion of words which by themselves would only serve to excite pride. Pious people make a great use of the mind, whereas mental exertion is of very little use, and is even antagonistic to true piety. We must make use only of that which God sends us to do or to suffer, and not forsake this divine reality to occupy our minds with the historical wonders of the divine work instead of gaining an increase of grace by our fidelity.

The marvels of this work, of which we read for the purpose of satisfying our curiosity, often only tend to disgust us with things that seem trifling but by which, if we do not despise them, the divine love effects very great things in us. Fools that we are! We admire and bless this divine action in the writings relating its history, and when it is ready to continue this writing on our hearts, we keep moving the paper and prevent it writing by our curiosity, to see what it is doing in and around us. Pardon, divine love, these defects; I can see them all in myself, for I am not yet able to understand how to let You act. So far I have not allowed myself to be cast into the mould. I have run through all Your workshops and have admired all Your works, but have not as yet, by abandonment, received even the bare outlines of Your pencil. Nevertheless I have found in You a kind Master, a Physician, a Father, a beloved Friend.

I will now become Your disciple, and will frequent no other school than Yours. Like the Prodigal Son I return hungering for Your bread. I relinquish the ideas which tend only to the satisfaction of mental curiosity; I will no longer run after masters and books but will only make use of them as of other things that present themselves, not for my own satisfaction, but in dependence on the divine action and in obedience to You. For love of You and to discharge my debts I will confine myself to the one essential business, that of the present moment, and thus enable You to act.

BOOK II

ON THE STATE OF ABANDONMENT

CHAPTER I.

ON THE NATURE AND EXCELLENCE OF THE STATE OF ABANDONMENT.

SECTION I.—*The life of God in the soul.*

There is a time when the soul lives in God, and a time when God lives in the soul. What is appropriate to one state is inconsistent with the other. When God lives in the soul it ought to abandon itself entirely to His providence. When the soul lives in God it is obliged to procure for itself carefully and very regularly, every means it can devise by which to arrive at the divine union. The whole procedure is marked out; the readings, the examinations, the resolutions. The guide is always at hand and everything is by rule, even the hours for conversation. When God lives in the soul it has nothing left of self, but only that which the spirit which actuates it imparts to it at each moment. Nothing is provided for the future, no road is marked out, but it is like a child which can be led wherever one pleases, and has only feeling to distinguish what is presented to it. No more books with marked passages for such a soul; often enough it is even deprived of a regular director, for God allows it no other support than that which He gives it Himself. Its dwelling is in darkness, forgetfulness, abandonment, death and nothingness. It feels keenly its wants and miseries without knowing from whence or when will come its relief. With eyes fixed on Heaven it waits peacefully and without anxiety for someone to come to its assistance. God, who finds no purer disposition in His spouse than this entire self-renunciation for the sake of living the life of grace according to the divine operation, provides her with necessary books, thoughts, insight into her own soul, advice and counsel, and the examples of the wise. Everything that others discover with great difficulty this soul finds in abandonment, and what they guard with care in order to be able to find it again, this soul receives at the moment there is occasion for it, and afterwards relinquishes so as to admit nothing but exactly what God desires it to have in order to live by Him alone. The former soul undertakes an infinity of good works for the glory of God, the latter is often cast aside in a corner of the world like a bit of broken crockery, apparently of no use to anyone. There, this soul, forsaken by creatures but in the enjoyment of God by a very real, true, and active love (active although infused in repose), does not attempt anything by its own impulse; it only knows that it has to abandon itself and to remain in the hands of God to be used by Him as He pleases. Often it is ignorant of its use, but God knows well. The world thinks it is useless, and appearances give colour to this judgment, but nevertheless it is very certain that in mysterious ways and by unknown channels, it spreads abroad an infinite amount of grace on persons who often have no idea of it, and of whom it never thinks. In souls abandoned to God everything is efficacious, everything is a sermon and apostolic. God imparts to their silence, to their repose, to their detachment, to their words, gestures, etc., a certain virtue which, unknown to them, works in the hearts of those around them; and, as they are guided by the occasional actions of others who are made use of by grace to instruct them without their knowledge, in the same way, they, in their turn, are made use of for the support and guidance of others without any direct acquaintance with them, or understanding to that effect.

God it is who works in them, by unexpected and often unknown impulses, so that these souls are like to Jesus, from whom proceeded a secret virtue for the healing of others. There is this difference between Him and them, that often they do not perceive the outflow of this virtue and even contribute nothing by co-operation: it is like a hidden balm, the perfume of which is exhaled without being recognised, and which knows not its own virtue.

SECTION II.—*The most perfect way.*

In this state the soul is guided by the divine action through every kind of obscurity.

When the soul is moved by the divine influence, it forsakes all works, practices, methods, means, books, ideas, and spiritual persons in order to be guided by God alone by abandoning itself to that moving power which becomes the sole source of its perfection. It remains in His hands like all the saints, understanding that the divine action alone can guide it in the right path, and that if it were to seek other means it would inevitably go astray in that unknown country which God compels it to traverse. It is, therefore, the action of God which guides and conducts souls by ways which it alone understands. It is, with these souls, like the changes of the wind. The direction is only known in the present moment, and the effects follow their causes by the will of God, which is only explained by these effects because it acts in these souls and makes them act either by hidden undoubted instincts, or by the duties of their state. This is all the spirituality they know; these are their visions and revelations, this is the whole of their wisdom and counsel insomuch that nothing is ever wanting to them. Faith makes them certain that what they do is well, whether they read, speak, or write; and if they take counsel it is only to be able to distinguish more clearly the divine action. All this is laid down for them and they receive it like the rest, beholding beneath these things the divine motive power and not fastening on the things presented, but using or leaving them, always leaning by faith on the infallible, unruffled, immutable and ever efficacious action of God at each moment. This they perceive and enjoy in all things, the least as well as the greatest, for it is entirely at their service at every moment. Thus they make use of things not because they have any confidence in them, or for their own sake, but in submission to the divine ordinance, and to that interior operation which, even under contrary appearances, they discover with equal facility and certitude. Their life, therefore, is spent, not in investigations or desires, weariness or sighs, but in a settled assurance of being in the most perfect way.

Every state of body or soul, and whatever happens interiorly or exteriorly as revealed at each moment to these souls is, to them, the fulness of the divine action, and the fulness of their joy. Created things are, to them, nothing but misery and dearth; the only true and just measure is in the working of the divine action. Thus, if it take away thoughts, words, books, food, persons, health, even life itself, it is exactly the same as if it did the contrary. The soul loves the divine action and finds it equally sanctifying under whatever shape it presents itself. It does not reason about the way it acts; it suffices for its approval that whatever comes is from this source.

SECTION III.—*Abandonment a Pledge of Predestination.*

The state of abandonment contains in itself pure faith, hope, and charity.

The state of abandonment is a certain mixture of faith, hope, and charity in one single act, which unites the soul to God and to His action. United, these three virtues together form but one in a single act, the raising of the heart to God, and abandonment to His action. But how can this divine mingling, this spiritual oneness be explained? How can a name be found to convey an idea of its nature, and to make the unity of this trinity intelligible? It can be explained thus. It is only by means of these three virtues that the possession and enjoyment of God and of His will can be attained. This adorable object is seen, is loved, and all things are hoped for from it. Either virtue can with equal justice be called pure love, pure hope, or pure faith, and if the state of which we are speaking is more frequently designated by the last name, it is not that the other theological virtues are excluded, but rather that they may be understood to subsist and to be practised in this state in obscurity.

There can be nothing more secure than this state in the things that are of God; nothing more disinterested than the character of the heart. On the side of God is the absolute certitude of faith, and on that of the heart is the same certitude tempered with fear and hope. O most desirable unity of the trinity of these holy virtues! Believe then, hope and love, but by a simple feeling which the Holy Spirit who is given you by God will produce in your soul. It is there that the unction of the name of God is diffused by the Holy Spirit in the centre of the heart. This is the word, this is the mystical revelation, and a pledge of predestination with all its happy results. "Quam bonus Israel Deus his qui recto sunt corde" (Psalm 72, i). This impress of the Holy Spirit in souls inflamed with His love, is called pure love on account of the torrent of delight overflowing every faculty, accompanied by a fulness of confidence and light; but in souls that are plunged in bitterness it is called pure faith because the darkness and obscurity of night are without alleviation. Pure love sees, feels, and believes. Pure faith believes without either seeing or feeling. In this is shown the difference between these two states, but this difference is only apparent, not real. The appearances are dissimilar, but in reality as the state of pure faith is not lacking in charity, neither is the state of pure love lacking in faith nor in abandonment; the terms being applied according to which virtue prevails. The different gradations of these virtues under the touch of the Holy Spirit form the variety of all supernatural and lofty states. And since God can rearrange them in an endless variety there is not a single soul that does not receive this priceless impress in a character suitable to it. The difference is nothing, there are the same faith, hope, and charity in all. Abandonment is a general means of receiving special virtues in every variety of different impresses. Souls cannot all lay claim to the same sort, nor to a similar state but all can be united to God, all can be abandoned to His action, all can receive the impress that is best suited to them, all in fact can live under the reign of God and enjoy a share in His justice with all its advantages. In this kingdom every soul can aspire to a crown, and whether a crown of love, or a crown of faith, it is always a crown, always the kingdom of God. There is this difference, it is true—the one is in light, the other in darkness; but again what does this signify if the soul belongs to God and obeys His will? We do not seek to know the name of this state, its characteristics, nor excellence, but we seek God alone and His action. The manner of it ought to be a matter of indifference to the soul. Let us therefore no

founded on the expectation of His protection, making everything pleasant and received with a good grace. It is indifference
to, and at the same time a preparation for every place, state, or
person. Faith is never unhappy even when the senses are most
desolate. This lively faith is always in God, always in His action
above contrary appearances by which the senses are darkened.
The senses, in terror, suddenly cry to the soul, "Unhappy one!
You have now no resource, you are lost," and instantly faith with
a stronger voice answers: "Keep firm, go on, and fear nothing."

SECTION V.—*The Great Merit of Pure Faith.*

By the state of abandonment and of pure faith the soul gains
more merit than by the most eminent good works.

Whatever we find extraordinary in the lives of the saints, such
as revelations, visions and interior locutions, is but a glimpse of
that excellence of their state which is contained and hidden in
the exercise of faith; because faith possesses all this by knowing
how to see and hear God in that which happens from moment
to moment. When these favours are manifested visibly it does
not mean that by faith they have not been already possessed, but
in order to make the excellence of faith visible for the purpose
of attracting souls to the practice of it; just as the glory of
Thabor, and the miracles of Jesus Christ were not from any
increase of His intrinsic excellence, but from the light which
from time to time escaped from the dark cloud of His humanity
to make it an object of veneration and love to others.

That which is wonderful in the saints is the constancy of their
faith under every circumstance; without this there would be no
sanctity. In the loving faith which makes them rejoice in God for
everything, their sanctity has no need of any extraordinary
manifestation; this could only prove useful to others who might
require the testimony of such signs; but the soul in this state,
happy in its obscurity, does in no way rely on these brilliant
manifestations; it allows them to show outwardly for the profit
of others, but keeps for itself what all have in common, the will
of God, and His good pleasure. Its faith is proved in hiding, and

not in manifesting itself, and those who require more proof have less faith.

Those who live by faith receive proofs, not as such, but as favours from the hand of God, and in this sense things that are extraordinary are not in contradiction to the state of pure faith.

But there are many saints whom God sets up for the salvation of souls, and from whose faces He causes rays of glory to stream for the enlightenment of the most blind. Of such were the Prophets and the Apostles and all those saints chosen by God to be set in the candlestick of the Church. There will ever be such, as there ever have been.

There is also an infinity of others who, having been created to shine in the heavens give no light in this world, but live and die in profound obscurity.

SECTION VI.—*Submission a Free Gift to God.*

The state of abandonment includes the merit of every separate operation.

Abandonment as practised interiorly contains every possible variety of operation, because, the soul giving itself up to the good pleasure of God, this surrender, effected by pure love, extends to all the operations of this good pleasure. Thus the soul practises at each moment an abandonment without limit, and in its virtue are comprehended all possible qualities and every method. It is, therefore, by no means the business of the soul to decide what is the object of the submission it owes to God; its sole occupation is to submit at all times and for all things.

What God requires of the soul is the essential part of abandonment. The free gifts He asks are abnegation, obedience, and love, the rest is His business. Provided that the soul carefully fulfils the duties of its state; provided it quietly follows the attraction given to it, and submits peacefully to the dealings of grace as to body and soul, it is in this way exercising interiorly one general and universal act, that of abandonment. This act is by no means limited by time, nor by the special duty of the moment, but possesses in the main all the merit and efficacy which a sincere good will always has, although the result does not depend upon it. What it desired to do is done, in the sight of God.

If God's good pleasure sets a limit to the exercise of particular faculties, it sets none to that of the will. The good pleasures of God, the being and essence of God are the objects of the will, and by the exercise of charity its union with God has neither limit, distinction, nor measure. If this charity ends in the exercise of the faculties for certain objects, it is because the will of God only goes so far; it contracts itself, so to speak, restricting itself to the exigencies of the present moment from whence it passes to the faculties, and then to the heart. Finding the heart pure, free, and without reserve, it communicates itself fully to it on account of the infinite capacity which charity has effected, by emptying it of all created things, thus rendering it capable of union with God. O heavenly purity! O blessed annihilation! O unreserved submission! through you is God drawn into the centre of the heart. Let the faculties then be what they will, provided, Lord, that I possess You. Do what You will with this insignificant creature; whether it works, becomes inspired, or becomes the subject of Your impressions, it is all one. All is yours, all is from You and for You. I have no longer anything to look after, anything to do. I have no hand in the arrangement of one single moment of my life, all is Yours. I ought neither to add to, nor to diminish anything, neither to seek after, nor to reflect upon, anything. It is for You to regulate everything. Direction, mortification, sanctity, perfection, and salvation are all Your business, Lord; mine is to be satisfied with Your work, and not to appropriate any action, or any state, but to leave all to Your good pleasure.

SECTION VII.—*Divine Favours Offered to All.*

Every soul is called to enjoy the infinite benefits contained in this state.

Therefore do I preach abandonment, and not any particular state. Every state in which souls are placed by Your grace is the same to me. I teach a general method by which all can attain the state which You have marked out for them. I do not exact more than the will to abandon themselves to Your guidance. You will make them arrive infallibly at the state which is best for them.

It is faith that I preach; abandonment, confidence, and faith; the will to be subject to, and to be the tool of the divine action, and to believe that at every moment this action is working in every circumstance, provided that the soul has more or less good-will. This is the faith that I preach. It is not a special kind of faith, nor of charity, but a general state by which all souls can find God under the different conditions which He assumes; and can take that form which divine grace has marked out for them. I have spoken to souls in trouble, and now I am speaking to all kinds of souls. It is the genuine instinct of my heart to care for all, to announce the saving secret far and wide, and to make myself all to all. In this happy disposition I make it a duty which I fulfil without difficulty, to weep with those who weep, to rejoice with those who rejoice, to speak foolishly with the foolish, and with the learned to make use of more learned and more scholastic terms. I wish to make all understand that although they cannot aspire to the same distinct favours, they can attain to the same love, the same abnegation, the same God and His work, and thence it follows naturally, to the highest sanctity. Those graces which are called extraordinary and are given as privileges to certain souls, are only so called because there are so few sufficiently faithful to become worthy of receiving them. This will be made manifest at the day of judgment. Alas! it will then be seen that instead of these divine favours having been withheld by God, it has been entirely by their own fault that these souls have been deprived of them. What untold blessings they would have received through the complete submission of a steadfast goodwill.

It is the same with regard to Jesus as with the divine action. If those who have no confidence in Him, nor respect for Him, do not receive any of the favours He offers to all, they have only their own bad disposition to thank for it. It is true that all cannot aspire to the same sublime states, to the same gifts, to the same degree of perfection; yet, if faithful to grace, they corresponded to it, each according to his degree, they would all be satisfied because they would all attain that degree of grace and of perfection which would fully satisfy their desires. They would be happy according to nature, and according to grace, because nature and grace share equally in the ardent desire for this priceless advantage.

SECTION VIII.—*God Reigns in a Pure Heart.*

All the treasures of grace are the fruit of purity of heart and perfect abandonment.

He, therefore, who wishes to enjoy an abundance of all blessings had but one thing to do; to purify his heart by detaching it from creatures, and to abandon himself entirely to God. In this purity and abandonment he will find all that he desires. "May others, Lord, ask You for all sorts of gifts, may they multiply their words and prayers; as for me, my God, I only ask one single gift, I have only one prayer to make—give me a pure heart." O pure heart! how happy you are; for by the liveliness of your faith you see God as He is in Himself. You see Him in all things and at every moment working within you and around you. In all things you are His subject and His instrument. He rules you and leads you. You have not to think because He thinks for you. Whatever happens to you, or may happen by His will, it is enough for Him that you will it also. He understands your readiness. In your salutary blindness you try to discover in yourself this desire, but you cannot see it, nevertheless He sees it quite clearly. How foolish you are! a well-disposed heart is a heart in which God dwells. Seeing therefore the good inclinations in this heart God well knows that it will remain always submissive to His will; He knows also that you are ignorant of what would be useful to you and therefore He makes it His business to give you what is necessary.

It matters very little to Him whether you are thwarted or not. You imagine you are going East, He makes you go West. You are about to strike against a rock, He pushes the tiller and brings you into port. Without either map or a compass, wind or tide, the voyages you make are always fortunate. If you encounter pirates, an unexpected puff of wind instantly wafts you beyond their reach.

O good will! O pure heart! Jesus well knew where to place you when He ranked you among the Beatitudes. What greater happiness can there be than to possess God, if He mutually possesses you? It is a state full of charm and of joy, in which the soul reposes peacefully in the bosom of divine Providence where it sports innocently with the divine Wisdom, feeling no anxiety about the journey which suffers no interruption, but in spite of rocks and pirates and constant storms, ever continues as happy as possible.

O pure heart! O good will! the sole foundation of every spiritual state, to you are granted the gifts of firm faith, holy hope, perfect confidence and pure love, and by you are they made profitable.

On your stem are grafted the flowers of the desert; in other words, from you spring those priceless graces which blossom in souls entirely detached, where God, as in an uninhabited dwelling, takes up His abode to the exclusion of all else. You are the faithful source from whence flow those streams that water the flower garden of the divine Spouse, and of His chosen one. Your voice calls all the souls of men saying to them, "Look well at me; it is I who impart fair love, that love which chooses the better part and lays hold of it. It is I who give birth to that fear, so gentle and efficacious, which produces a horror of evil, and makes it easy to avoid; I, who bring to light those fine perceptions by which are discovered the greatness of God and the value of virtue; in fine it is from me that those ardent desires take their rise, enkindled by holy hope. It is I who cause virtue to be practised in expectation of the promised reward—that divine Object of our love, the possession of Whom will one day form the happiness of faithful souls. Invite them all to come to you to be enriched with your inexhaustible treasures. All spiritual states and paths lead back to you. It is from you that they derive all that is beautiful, attractive, and charming, for all is drawn from your depths. Those marvellous fruits of grace, and of every kind of virtue that helps to nourish the soul, and that abounds on every side, are produced by you. Milk and honey flow in your land. Your breasts distil milk, and on your bosom is the bouquet of myrrh from which, under the pressure of your fingers, the aromatic liquid flows abundantly.

Let us go, then, let us run and fly to that ocean of love by which we are attracted! What are we waiting for? Let us start at once, let us lose ourselves in God, even in His heart, to become inebriated with the wine of His charity. We shall find in His heart the key of heavenly treasures. Let us begin at once our journey to Heaven. There is no passage that we cannot discover, nothing is shut against us, neither the garden, nor the cellar, nor the vineyard. If we desire to breathe the fresh country air, we can go on our own feet and return when we please. With this key of David we can enter and depart; it is the key of science, and of that abyss in which are contained all the hidden treasures of divine Wisdom. With this heavenly key we also open the gates of mystical death with its sacred darkness. By it also we descend into the deep pools and into the den of lions. By it souls are thrust into those obscure prisons from whence they emerge unscathed. By it we are introduced into that joyful place where light and understanding have their dwelling, where the Spouse takes the midday rest in the open air, and where He reveals the secrets of His love to faithful souls. O divine incommunicable secrets that no mortal tongue can describe! Since every good thing that it is possible to possess is given to those who love, let us love then, in order to be enriched with them; for love produces sanctity with all that accompanies it. It flows on every side, on the right hand and on the left, into those hearts open to receive this divine outpouring. O divine harvest for eternity! it is not possible to praise you sufficiently. And why speak so much about you? How much better to possess you in silence than to praise you with mere words. But what am I saying? You must be praised but only because you take possession of us, for, from the moment you enter into possession of a heart, then reading, writing, speaking or silence are matters of complete indifference. One can take or leave anything, live in solitude, or as an apostle; one is well or ill, dull or eloquent, in fact anything that you will. That which you dictate, your faithful echo, the heart, repeats to all the faculties. In that compound of matter and spirit, the heart, which you regard as your kingdom, you reign supreme, and as it has no other instincts than those which you inspire, all the things that you present are equally agreeable. Those things that nature, or the devil wish to substitute, cause nothing but disgust and horror. If you allow it to be occasionally overcome, it is only to make it wiser and more humble; but from the moment it realises its mistake it returns to you with renewed love, and clings to you with greater tenacity.

CHAPTER II.

SECTION I.—*Sacrifice, the Foundation of Sanctity.*

The first great duty of souls called by God to this state is the absolute and entire surrender of themselves to Him.

"Sacrificate sacrificium, et sperate in Domino." That is to say that the great and solid foundation of the spiritual life is the sacrifice of oneself to God, subjecting oneself to His good pleasure in all things, both interior and exterior, and becoming so completely forgetful of self thereafter as to regard oneself as a chattel, sold and delivered, to which one no longer has any right. In this way the good pleasure of God forms one's whole felicity; and His happiness, glory and existence one's sole good. This foundation laid, the soul has nothing else to do but to rejoice that God is God, and to abandon itself so entirely to His good pleasure that it feels an equal satisfaction in whatever it does, nor ever reflects on the uses to which it is applied by the arrangements of this good pleasure. To abandon oneself, therefore, is the principal duty to be fulfilled, involving, as it does, the faithful discharge of all the obligations of one's state. The perfection with which these duties are accomplished will be the measure of the sanctity of each individual soul. A saintly soul is a soul freely submissive, with the help of grace, to the divine will. All that follows on this free consent is the work of God, and not of man. The soul should blindly abandon itself and be indifferent about everything. This is all that God requires of it, and as to the rest He determines and chooses according to His own

61

plans, as an architect selects and arranges the stones for the building he is about to construct. It is therefore of the first importance to love God and His will, and to love this will in whatever way it is made manifest to us, without desiring anything else. The soul has no concern in the choice of different objects, that is God's affair, and whatever He gives is best for the soul. The whole of spirituality is an abridgment of this maxim, "Abandon yourself entirely to the over-ruling of God, and by self-oblivion be eternally occupied in loving and serving Him without any of those fears, reflexions, examens, and anxieties which the affair of our salvation, and perfection sometimes occasion." Since God wishes to do all for us, let us place everything in His hands once and for all, leaving them to His infinite wisdom; and trouble no more about anything but what concerns Him. On then, my soul, on with head uplifted above earthly things, always satisfied with God, with everything He does, or makes you do. Take good care not to imprudently entertain a crowd of anxious reflexions which, like so many trackless ways, carry our footsteps far and wide until we are hopelessly astray. Let us go through that labyrinth of self-love by leaping over it, instead of traversing its interminable windings.

On, my soul, through despondency, illness, aridity, uncertain tempers, weakness of disposition, snares of the devil and of men; through suspicions, jealousies, evil imaginations and prejudices. Let us soar like the eagle above all these clouds with eyes always fixed on the sun, and on its ways, which represent our obligations. All this we must needs feel, but we must, at the same time, remember that ours is not a life of mere sentiment, and that it does not depend upon us either to feel, or to be callous. Let us live in the higher regions of the soul in which God and His will form an eternity ever equal, ever the same, ever unchanging. In this dwelling entirely spiritual, wherein the uncreated, immeasurable and ineffable holds the soul at an infinite distance from all that is specific in shadows and created atoms, it remains calm, even when the senses are tossed about by tempests. It has become independent of the senses; their troubles and agitations and innumerable vicissitudes no more affect it, than the clouds that obscure the sky for a moment and then fade away, affect the sun. We know that all passes away like clouds blown along by the wind, and nothing is consecutive nor ordered, but everything is in a state of perpetual change. In the state of faith, as in that of glory, God and His will is the eternal object that captivates the heart, and will one day form its true happiness, and this glorious state of the soul will influence the material part which at present is the prey of monsters and savage beasts. Beneath these appearances, terrible though they be, the divine action will so work on this material part as to make it partake of a heavenly power which will render it brilliant as the sun; for the faculties of the sensitive soul, and those of the body are prepared here below like gold or iron, or like canvas for a picture, or stones for a building. Like the matter of which these different materials are composed they will not attain their brilliance and purity of form until they have passed through many alterations, have endured many deprivations, and survived many destructions. Whatever they suffer here below under the hand of God serves to that end.

The soul, in the state of faith, which knows the secret of God, dwells always in peace. All that takes place interiorly, instead of alarming, reassures it. Deeply convinced that it is guided by God, it takes all that happens as so much grace, and overlooking the instrument with which God works, it thinks only of the work that He is doing.

It is actuated by love to fulfil faithfully and exactly all its duties. All that is distinct in a soul abandoned to God, is the work of grace, with the exception of those defects which are slight, and which the action of grace even turns to good account. I call that distinct of which a soul receives a sensible impression either of sorrow or consolation through those things applied to it unceasingly by the divine will for its improvement. I call it distinct because it is more clearly distinguished by the soul from all else that takes place within it. In all these things faith sees only God, and applies itself solely to become conformed to His will.

SECTION II.—*The Pains and Consolations of Abandonment.*

The soul ought to strip itself of all things created in order to arrive at the state of abandonment.

This state is full of consolation for those who have attained it; but to do so it is necessary to pass through much anguish. The doctrine concerning pure love can only be taught by the action of God, and not by any effort of the mind. God teaches the soul by pains and obstacles, not by ideas.

This science is a practical knowledge by which God is enjoyed as the only good. In order to master this science it is necessary to be detached from all personal possessions, to gain this detachment, to be really deprived of them. Therefore it is only by constant crosses, and by a long succession of all kinds of mortifications, trials, and deprivations, that pure love becomes established in the soul. This must continue until all things created become as though they did not exist, and God becomes all in all. To effect this God combats all the personal affections of the soul, so that when these take any especial shape, such as some pious notion, some help to devotion; or when there is any idea of being able to attain perfection by some such method, or such a path or way, or by the guidance of some particular person; in fine to whatever the soul attaches itself, God upsets its plans, and allows it to find, instead of success in these projects, nothing but confusion, trouble, emptiness, and folly. Hardly has it said "I must go this way, I must consult this person, or, I must act in such a manner," than God immediately says the exact contrary, and withdraws all the virtue usual in the means adopted by the soul. Thus, finding only deception and emptiness in everything, the soul is compelled to have recourse to God Himself, and to be content with Him.

Happy the soul that understands this lovingly severe conduct of God, and that corresponds faithfully with it. It is raised above all that passes away to repose in the immutable and the infinite. It is no longer dissipated among created things by giving them love and confidence, but allows them only when it becomes a duty to do so, or when enjoined by God, and when His will is made especially manifest in the matter. It inhabits a region above earthly abundance or dearth, in the fulness of God who is its permanent good. God finds this soul quite empty of its own inclinations, of its own movements, of its own choice. It is a dead subject, and shrouded in universal indifference. The whole of the divine Being, coming thus to fill the heart, casts over all created things a shadow, as of nothingness, absorbing all their distinctions and all their varieties. Thus there remains neither efficacy, nor virtue in anything created, and the heart is neither drawn towards, nor has any inclination for created things, because the majesty of God fills it to its utmost extent. Living in God in this way, the heart becomes dead to all else, and all is dead to it. It is for God, who gives life to all things, to revive the soul with regard to His creation, and to give a different aspect to all things in the eyes of the soul. It is the order of God which is this life. By this order the heart goes out towards the creature as far as is necessary or useful, and it is also by this order that the creature is carried towards the soul and is accepted by it. Without this divine virtue of the good pleasure of God, things created are not admitted by the soul, neither is the soul at all inclined towards them. This dissolution of all things as far as the soul is concerned, and then, by the will of God, their being brought once more into existence, compels the soul at each moment to see God in all things, for each moment is spent for the satisfaction of God only, and in an unreserved self-abandonment with regard to its relations to all possible created things, or rather to those created, or possibly to be created by the order of God. Therefore each moment contains all.

SECTION III.—*The Different Duties of Abandonment.*

The active exercise of abandonment either in relation to precept, or to inspiration.

Although souls called by God to a state of abandonment are much more passive than active, yet they cannot expect to be exempted from all activity. This state being nothing else but the virtue of abandonment exercised more habitually, and with greater perfection, should, like this virtue, be composed of two kinds of duty; the active accomplishment of the divine will, and the passive acceptance of all that this will pleases to send.

It consists essentially, as we have already said, in the gift of our whole self to God to be used as He thinks fit. Well! the good pleasure of God makes use of us in two ways; either it compels us to perform certain actions, or it simply works within us. We, therefore, submit also in two ways, either by the faithful accomplishment of its clearly defined orders, or else by a simple and passive submission to its impressions of either pleasure or pain. Abandonment implies all this, being nothing else but a perfect submission to the order of God as made manifest at the present moment. It matters little to the soul in what manner it is obliged to abandon itself, and what the present moment contains; all that is absolutely necessary is that it should abandon itself unreservedly. There are, then, prescribed duties to be fulfilled, and necessary duties to be accepted, and further there is a third kind which also forms part of active fidelity, although it does not properly belong to works of precept. In this are comprised inspired duties; those to which the spirit of God inclines the hearts that are submissive to Him. The accomplishment of this kind of duty requires a great simplicity, a gentle and cheerful heartiness, a soul easily moved by every breath of directing grace; for there is nothing else to do but to give oneself up, and to obey its inspirations simply and freely. So that souls may not be deceived, God never fails to give them wise guidance to indicate with what liberty or reserve these inspirations should be made use of. The third kind of duty takes precedence of all law, formalities, or marked-out rules. It is what, in saints, appears singular and extraordinary; it is what regulates their vocal prayer, interior words, the perception of their faculties, and also all that makes their lives noble, such as austerities, zeal, and the prodigality of their self-devotion for others. As all this belongs to the interior rule of the Holy Spirit, no one ought to try to obtain it, to imagine that they have it, to desire it, nor to regret that they do not possess the grace to undertake this kind of work, and to practise these uncommon virtues, because they are only really meritorious when practised according to the direction of God. If one is not content with this reserve one lays oneself open to the influence of one's own ideas, and will become exposed to illusion.

It is necessary to remark that there are souls that God keeps hidden and little in their own eyes, and in the eyes of others. Far from giving them striking qualities, His design for them is that they should remain in obscurity. They would be deceived if they desired to attempt a different way. If they are well instructed they will recognise that fidelity to their nothingness is their right path, and they will find peace in their lowliness. The only difference, therefore, in their way and that of, apparently, more favoured souls, is the difference they make for themselves by the amount of their love and submission to the will of God; for, if they surpass in these virtues the souls that appear to work more than they exteriorly, their sanctity is, without doubt, so much the greater. This shows that each soul ought to content itself with the duties of its state, and the over-ruling of Providence; clearly God exacts this equally from all. As to attraction and the impressions received by the soul, these are given by God alone to whom He pleases. One must not try to produce them oneself, nor to make efforts to increase them. Natural effort is in direct opposition and quite contrary to infused inspirations, which should come in peace. The voice of the divine Spouse will awaken the soul, which should only proceed according to the inspirations of the Holy Spirit, for, if it were to act according to its own ideas it would make no progress.

Therefore, if it should feel neither attraction nor grace to do those things that make the saints so much admired, it must, in justice to itself, say, "God has willed it thus for the saints, but not for me."

SECTION IV.—*God Does All for a Soul of Goodwill.*

The conduct of a soul raised to a state of abandonment with regard to this twofold manifestation of the good pleasure of God.

Souls called by God to a life of perfect abandonment resemble in this respect our Lord, His holy Mother, and St. Joseph.

The will of God was, to them, the fulness of life. Submitting entirely to this will as to precept and inspiration directly it was made manifest to them, they were always in complete dependence on, what we might call, the purely providential will of God. From this it follows that their lives, although extraordinary in perfection, showed outwardly nothing that is not common to all, and quite ordinary. They fulfilled the duties of religion, and of their state as others do, and in, apparently, the same way. For the rest, if one scrutinizes their conduct, nothing can be discovered either striking or peculiar; all follows the same course of ordinary events. That which might single them out is not discernible; it is that dependence on the supreme will which arranges all things for them, and in which they habitually live. The divine will confers on them a complete self-mastery on account of the habitual submission of their hearts.

Therefore the souls in question are, by their state, both solitary and free; detached from all things in order to belong to God, to love Him in peace, and to fulfil faithfully the present duty according to His expressed will. They do not allow themselves to reflect, to neglect, nor to think of consequences, causes or reasons; it is enough for them to go on simply, accomplishing their plain duties just as if there did not exist for them anything but their present obligation, and their duty to God. The present moment, then, is like a desert in which the soul sees only God whom it enjoys; and is only occupied about those things which He requires of it, leaving and forgetting all else, and abandoning it to Providence. This soul, like an instrument, neither receives interiorly more than the operation of God effects passively, nor gives exteriorly more than this same operation applies actively.

This interior application is accompanied by a free and active co-operation which is, at the same time, infused and mystical; that is to say that God, finding in this soul all the necessary qualifications for acting according to His laws, and satisfied with its goodwill, spares it the trouble of doing so, by bestowing all that would otherwise be the fruit of its efforts, or of its effectual goodwill. It is as though someone, seeing a friend preparing for a troublesome journey, would go in his stead, so that the friend would have the intention of going, but he spared the trouble of the journey; yet by this impersonation he would have gone himself, at least virtually. This journey would be free because it would be the result of a free determination taken beforehand to please the friend who then takes upon himself the trouble and expense; it would also be active because it will be a real advance; and it will be interior because effected without outward activity; and, finally, it will be mystical because of the hidden principle it contains. But to return to that kind of co-operation that we have explained by this imaginary journey; you will observe that it is entirely different from fidelity in the fulfilment of obligations. The work of fulfilling these is neither mystical nor infused, but free and active as commonly understood. Therefore abandonment to the good pleasure of God contains activity as well as passivity. In it there is nothing of self, but an habitual general goodwill, which like an instrument, has no action of itself, but responds to the touch of the master. While in his hands it fulfils all the purposes for which it was formed. Intentional and determined obedience to the will of God is, in the ordinary order of vigilance, care, attention, prudence, and discretion; although ordinary efforts are sensibly aided, or begun by grace. Leaving God, then, to act for all the rest, reserve for yourself at the present moment, only love and obedience, which virtues the soul will practise eternally. This love, infused into the soul in silence, is a real action of which it makes a perpetual obligation. It ought, in fact, to preserve it faithfully, and to maintain itself constantly in those dispositions resulting from it, all of which, it is evident, cannot be done without action. The action, however, is quite different to obedience to the present duty, by which the soul so disposes its faculties as to fulfil perfectly the will of God made manifest to it exteriorly, without expecting anything extraordinary.

This divine will is to the soul in all things its method, its rule, and its direct and safe way. It is an unalterable law which is of all times, of all places, and of all states. It is a straight line which the soul must follow with courage and fidelity, neither diverging to the right, nor to the left, nor overstepping the bounds. Whatever is over and above must be received passively, as it carries on its work in abandonment. In a word, the soul is active in all that the present duty requires, but passive and submissive in all the rest, about which there should be no self-will, but patient waiting for the divine motion.

SECTION V.—*The Common Way for all Souls.*

The soul that aims at union with God should value all the operations of His grace, but should only attach itself to that of the present moment.

It is by union with the will of God that we enjoy and possess Him; and it is an illusion to endeavour to obtain this divine enjoyment by any other means. Union with the will of God is the universal means. It does not act by one method only, but all methods and all ways are, by its virtue, sanctified. The divine will unites God to our souls in many different ways, and that which suits us is always best for us. All ways should be esteemed and loved, because in each we should behold that which is ordained by God accommodating itself to each individual soul, and selecting the most suitable method of effecting by it the divine union. The duty of the soul is to submit to this choice, and to make none for itself; and this without dispensing itself from esteeming and loving this adorable will in its work in others. For instance, if this divine will should prevent me saying vocal prayers, having sensible devotion, or receiving lights on mysteries, I should still love and esteem the silence and bareness induced by the sight of the faith of others; while for myself I should make use of the present moment, and by it should become united to God. I should not, as the Quietists do, reduce all religion to personal inaction despising all other means; because what makes perfection is obedience to the law of God which always renders the means it applies suitable to the soul. No! I should not admit of obstacles or bounds to the will of God, neither should I take anything in place of it, but should welcome it in whatever way it was made manifest to me, and should revere it in whatever way it was pleased to unite itself to others. Thus all ordinary souls have but one common way in which each is distinct and different in order to form the variety of the mystical robe of the Church. All these souls mutually approve of, and esteem each other, and all say "We are going to the same goal by different paths, and are all united in the same way, and by the same means in the ordinance of God, which is so different in each." It is in this sense that we must read the lives of the saints, and other spiritual books, without ever making a change, and forsaking our own path. For this reason it is necessary that we should neither read spiritual books, nor hold spiritual conversation unless God so will; for, if He makes it the duty of the present moment, the soul, far from making any change will be strengthened in its way, either by what it finds in conformity with its own method, or even by that in which it differs. But if the will of God does not make this reading, or spiritual intercourse a present duty it will cause nothing but trouble, and a confusion of ideas; and a succession of changes will ensue; because without the concurrence of God's will there cannot be order in anything.

Since when, therefore, have we busied ourselves with the pains and anxieties of our souls which have nothing to do with our present duty? When will God be all in all to us? Let creatures act according to their nature, but let nothing hinder us, let us go beyond all created things and live entirely for God.

SECTION VI.—*The Duty of the Present Moment the Only Rule.*

From souls in this state God exacts the most perfect docility to the action of His grace.

It is necessary to be detached from all that one feels, and from all that one does, to follow this method, by which one subsists in God alone, and in the present duty. All regard to what is beyond this should be cut off as superfluous. One must restrict oneself to the present duty without thinking of the preceding one, or of the one which is to follow. I imagine the law of God to be always before you, and that the practice of abandonment has rendered your soul docile to the divine action. You feel some impulse that makes you say, "I have a drawing towards this person"; or "I have an inclination to read a certain book, to receive, or to give certain advice, to complain of certain things, to open my mind to another, or to receive confidence; to give away something, or to perform some action." Well! obey this impulse according to the inspiration of grace without stopping to reflect, to reason, or to make efforts. Give yourself up to these things for as long as God wishes without doing so through any self-will. In the state in question the will of God is shown to us because He dwells within us. This will ought to supplant all our usual supports. At each moment we have to practise some virtue. To this the obedient soul is faithful; nothing of what it has learnt by reading, or hearing is forgotten, and the most mortified novice could not fulfil her duties better. It is for this that these souls are attracted sometimes to one book, sometimes to another; or else to make some remark, some reflexion on what may seem but a trifling circumstance. At one time God gives them the attraction to learn something that at some future time will encourage them in the practice of virtue. Whatever these souls do, they do because they feel an attraction for it, without knowing why. All they can explain on the subject can be reduced to this: "I feel myself drawn to write, to read, to ask, to examine this; I follow this attraction, and God who gives it to me keeps these particular things in reserve in my faculties to become in future the nucleus of other attractions which will become useful to myself and others." This is what makes it necessary for these souls to be simple, gentle, yielding, and submissive to the faintest breath of these scarcely perceptible impressions.

In the state of abandonment the only rule is the duty of the present moment. In this the soul is light as a feather, liquid as water, simple as a child, active as a ball in receiving and following all the inspirations of grace. Such souls have no more consistence and rigidity than molten metal. As this takes any form according to the mould into which it is poured, so these souls are pliant and easily receptive of any form that God chooses to give them. In a word, their disposition resembles the atmosphere, which is affected by every breeze; or water, which flows into any shaped vessel exactly filling every crevice. They are before God like a perfectly woven fabric with a clear surface;

and neither think, nor seek to know what God will be pleased to trace thereon, because they have confidence in Him, they abandon themselves to Him, and, entirely absorbed by their duty, they think not of themselves, nor of what may be necessary for them, nor of how to obtain it. The more assiduously do they apply themselves to their little work, so simple, so hidden, so secret, and outwardly contemptible, the more does God embroider and embellish it with brilliant colours. On the surface of this simple canvas of love and obedience His hand traces the most beautiful design, the most delicate, and intricate pattern, the most divine figures. "Mirificavit Dominus sanctum suum." "The Lord hath made His holy one wonderful" (Psalm iv). It is true that a canvas simply and blindly given up to the work of the pencil only feels its movement at each moment. Each blow of the hammer on the chisel can only produce one cruel mark at a time, and the stone struck by repeated blows cannot know, nor see the form produced by them. It only feels that it is being diminished, filed, cut, and altered by the chisel. And a stone that is destined to become a crucifix or a statue without knowing it, if it were asked, "What is happening to you?" would reply if it could speak, "Do not ask me, I only know one thing, and that is, to remain immovable in the hands of my master, to love him, and to endure all that he inflicts upon me. As for the end for which I am destined, it is his business to understand how it is to be accomplished; I am as ignorant of what he is doing as of what I am destined to become; all I know is that his work is the best, and the most perfect that could be, and I receive each blow of the chisel as the most excellent thing that could happen to me, although, truth to tell, each blow, in my opinion, causes the idea of ruin, destruction, and disfigurement. But that is not my affair; content with the present moment, I think of nothing but my duty, and I endure the work of this clever master without knowing, or occupying myself about it."

Yes! give to God what belongs to Him, and remain lovingly passive in his hands. Hold for certain that what takes place either exteriorly or interiorly is best for you.

Allow God to act, and abandon yourself to Him. Let the

chisel perform its office, the needle do its work. Let the brush of the artist cover the canvas with many tints which only have the appearance of daubs. Correspond with all these divine operations by a simple and constant submission, a forgetfulness of self, and an assiduous application to duty. Continue thus in your own groove without studying the way, the ins and outs, and surroundings, the names or particulars of the places; go on blindly pursuing this path, and you will be shown what is to follow. Seek only the kingdom of God and His justice by love and obedience, and all the rest will be added to you. We meet with many souls who are distressed about themselves, and inquire anxiously, "Who will direct us so that we may become mortified and holy, and attain perfection?" Let them search in books for the description and characteristics of this marvellous work, its nature and qualities; but as for you, do you remain peacefully united to God by love, and follow blindly the clear straight path of duty. The angels are at your side during this time of darkness, and they will bear you up. If God requires more of you, He will make it known to you by His inspirations.

SECTION VII.—*Trust in the Guidance of God.*

The docile soul will not seek to learn by what road God is conducting it.

When God makes Himself the guide of a soul He exacts from it an absolute confidence in Him, and a freedom from any sort of disquietude as to the way in which He conducts it. This soul, therefore, is urged on without perceiving the path traced out before it. It does not imitate either what it has seen, or what it has read, but proceeds by its own action, and cannot do otherwise without grave risk. The divine action is ever fresh, it never retraces its steps, but always marks out new ways. Souls that are conducted by it never know where they are going; their ways are neither to be found in books, nor in their own minds; the divine action carries them step by step, and they progress only according to its movement.

When you are conducted by a guide who takes you through

an unknown country at night across fields where there are no
tracks, by his own skill, without asking advice from anyone, or
giving you any inkling of his plans; how can you choose but
abandon yourself? Of what use is it looking about to find out
where you are, to ask the passers-by, or to consult maps and
travellers? The plans or fancies of a guide who insists on being
trusted would not allow of this. He would take pleasure in over-
coming the anxiety and distrust of the soul, and would insist on
an entire surrender to his guidance. If one is convinced that he
is a good guide one must have faith in him, and abandon oneself
to his care.

The divine action is essentially good; it does not need to be
reformed or controlled. It began at the creation of the world,
and to the present time has manifested ever fresh energy. Its
operations are without limit, its fecundity inexhaustible. It acted
in one way yesterday, to-day it acts differently. It is the same
action applied at each moment to produce ever new effects, and
it will extend from eternity to eternity. It has produced Abel,
Noah, Abraham, all different types; Isaac, also original, and
Jacob from no copy; neither does Joseph follow any prefigure.
Moses has no prototype among his progenitors. David and the
Prophets are quite apart from the Patriarchs. St. John the
Baptist stands alone. Jesus Christ is the first-born; the Apostles
act more by the guidance of His spirit than in imitation of His
works.

Jesus Christ did not set a limit for Himself, neither did He
follow all His own maxims to the letter. The Holy Spirit ever
inspired His holy soul and, being entirely abandoned to its every
breath, it had no need to consult the moment that had passed,
to know how to act in that which was coming. The breath of
grace shaped every moment according to the eternal truths sub-
sisting in the invisible and unfathomable wisdom of the Blessed
Trinity. The soul of Jesus Christ received these directions at
every moment, and acted upon them externally. The Gospel
shows in the life of Jesus Christ a succession of these truths; and
this same Jesus who lives and works always, continues to live and
work in the souls of His saints.

If you would live according to the Gospel, abandon yourself

simply and entirely to the action of God. Jesus Christ is its supreme mouthpiece. "He was yesterday, is to-day, and will be for ever." (Hebr. xiii, 8); continuing, not recommencing His life. What He has done is finished; what remains to be done is being carried on at every moment. Each saint receives a share in this divine life, and in each, Jesus Christ is different, although the same in Himself. The life of each saint is the life of Jesus Christ; it is a new gospel. The cheeks of the spouse are compared to beds of flowers, to gardens filled with fragrant blossoms. The divine action is the gardener, admirably arranging the flower beds. This garden resembles no other, for among all the flowers there are no two alike, or that can be described as being of the same species, except in the fidelity with which they respond to the action of the Creator, in leaving Him free to do as He pleases, and, on their side, obeying the laws imposed on them by their nature. Let God act, and let us do what He requires of us; this is the Gospel; this is the general Scripture, and the common law.

SECTION VIII.—*Great Faith is Necessary.*

This total abandonment is as simple as its effects are marvellous.

Such then is the straight path to sanctity. Such is the state of perfection, and of the duties imposed by it; such the great and incomparable secret of abandonment; a secret that is, in reality, no secret, an art without art.

God, who exacts it of all, has explained it clearly, and made it intelligible, and quite simple. What is obscure in the way of pure faith is not necessary for the soul in that way, to practise; there is, in fact, nothing more easy to understand, nor more luminous; the mystery is only in what is done by God.

This is what takes place in the Blessed Eucharist. That which is necessary to change bread into the Body of Jesus Christ, is so clear and so easy that the most ignorant priest is capable of doing it; yet it is the mystery of mysteries, where all is so hidden, so obscure, so incomprehensible that the more spiritual and enlightened one is, the more faith is required to believe it. The way of pure faith presents much that is similar. Its effect is to enable one to find God at each moment; it is this that makes it so exalted, so mystical, so blessed. It is an inexhaustible fund of thought, of discourse, of writing, it is a whole collection, and source of wonders. To produce so prodigious an effect but one thing is necessary; to let God act, and to do all that He wills according to one's state. Nothing in the spiritual life could be easier, nor more within the power of everyone; and yet nothing could be more wonderful, nor any path more obscure. To walk in it the soul has need of great faith, all the more so as reason is always suspicious, and has always some argument against it. All its ideas are confused. There is nothing in it that reason has ever known or read about, or been accustomed to admire; it is something quite new. "The Prophets were saints, but this Jesus is a sorcerer," said the Jews. If the soul following their example, is scandalised, it shows but little faith, and well deserves to be deprived of those wonderful things that God is so ready to work in the faithful soul.

CHAPTER III.

SECTION I.—*Unwise Interference.*

The first trial: the obloquy and unreasonable exactions of persons with a reputation for wisdom and piety.

There is no way more secure than that of abandonment, and none more easy, sweet, clear, and less subject to illusion and error. In it God is loved and all Christian duties fulfilled; the Sacraments are frequented, and all the exterior acts of religion which are binding to all are performed. Superiors are obeyed, and the duties of the state of life are discharged; temptations of the flesh, the world, and the devil are continually resisted; for none are more on guard, or more vigilant in acquitting themselves of all their obligations, than those who follow this way.

If this is the case, why is it that they should be subject to so many contradictions? The most usual of these is, that when they, like other Christians, have accomplished all that the most strict theologian could exact, they are expected also to be bound to inconvenient practices to which the Church by no means obliges them; and if they do not comply they are charged with labouring under illusion. But I ask, can a Christian who confines himself to the observance of God's commandments, and those of the Church, and who, besides, without practising meditation, contemplation, or spiritual reading, and without being attached to any particular form of devotion, yet attends to worldly business, and to other affairs of private life—can he be wrong? One cannot presume to accuse, or even to suspect him of error. One must admit this to oneself, and while leaving the Christian of whom I am speaking in peace, it is but justice not to trouble a soul that not only fulfils the precepts at least as well as one does oneself, but whom in addition, practises exterior acts of piety that are even unknown to others, or, if known, are treated with indifference. Prejudice goes so far as to affirm that this soul deceives itself, and deludes itself because, after having submitted to all that the Church prescribes, it holds itself free to be in the condition to give itself without hindrance to the interior operations of God, and to attend to the impressions of His grace at times when no other duty intervenes to expressly compel them. In a word they are condemned because they employ that time which others give to amusements and temporal affairs, in loving God. Is not this a crying injustice? This cannot be too strongly insisted upon. If anyone keeps the ordinary course, goes to confession once a year, nothing is said about it, he is left in peace with an occasional injunction, not pressed with too much importunity, nor making it an obligation, to do a little more. If he should change his ways and try to improve them, then he is overwhelmed with counsels for his conduct, and with different methods; and if he does not follow these pious rules diligently, then he is done for, he is a subject of suspicion, and nothing is too bad to predict of him.

Are they not aware that these practices, however good and holy they may be, are, after all, only a way leading to divine union? Is it necessary, then, to be always on the road when one has already arrived at the goal.

Nevertheless, it is this that is exacted of a soul which is supposed to be labouring under illusion. This soul has made its way, like others, at the beginning; like them it knew what to do, and did it faithfully; it would be vain now to attempt to keep it bound to the same practices. Since God, moved by the efforts it has made to advance with these helps, has taken it on Himself to lead it to this happy union, from the time it arrived at the state of abandonment, and by love possessed God; in fine, from the time that the God of all goodness, relieving it of all its trouble and industry, made Himself the principle of its operations, these first methods lost all their value and were but the road it had traversed. To insist upon these methods being resumed and constantly followed, would be to make the soul forsake the end at which it had arrived to re-enter the way which led to it. But, if this soul has any experience, their time and trouble will be thrown away. In vain will they pursue it with noisy clamours; turning a deaf ear it will remain untroubled and unmoved in that intimate peace in which it so advantageously exercises its love. This is the centre in which it reposes, or, if you prefer it, it is the straight line traced by the hand of God. It will continue to walk therein, for all its duties are plainly marked out in it and by following this line it fulfils them without confusion or haste as they present themselves. For all else it holds itself in perfect liberty, always ready to obey every movement of grace directly it perceives it, and to abandon itself to the care of Providence. God makes known to this soul that He intends to be its Master, and to direct it by His grace; and makes it understand that it cannot, without attacking the sovereign rights of its Creator, allow its own liberty to be fettered. It feels that, if it tied itself down, to the rules of those who live by their own efforts and industry, instead of acting according to the attraction of grace, it would be deprived of many things necessary in order to be able to fulfil future duties. But, as no one knows this, it is judged and condemned for its simplicity, and, though it does not find fault with others but approves of every state, and well knows how to discern every degree of progress, it is despised by pretended wiseacres who cannot appreciate this sweet and hearty submission to divine Providence.

Worldly wisdom cannot understand the perpetual wanderings of the Apostles, who did not settle anywhere. Ordinary spirituality also cannot endure that souls should depend for their action on divine Providence. There are but few in this state who approve of them, but God, who instructs men by means of their fellow creatures, never fails to make such souls encounter those who abandon themselves to Him with simplicity and fidelity. Besides, these latter require less direction than others in consequence of having attained to this state with the help of very good directors. If they find that they are occasionally left to themselves, it is because divine Providence removes by death, or banishes by some event, the guides who have led them in this way. Even then, they are always willing to be guided, and only wait in peace the moment arranged by Providence. During the time of privation also, they meet from time to time persons in whom they feel they can repose a confidence inspired by God, although they know nothing about them. This is a sign that He makes use of them to communicate certain lights, even if these are only temporary. These souls ask advice, therefore, and when it is given they follow it with the greatest docility. In default of such assistance however, they have recourse to the maxims supplied to them by their first directors. Thus they are always very well directed, either by the old principles formerly received, or by the advice of those directors they encounter, and they make use of all until God sends them persons in whom they can confide, and who will show them His Will.

SECTION II.—*Unjust Judgments.*

Second trial of the state of abandonment. The apparent uselessness and exterior defects allowed by God in the souls He wills to raise to this state.

The second trial of souls conducted by God in this way is the result of their apparent uselessness, and of their exterior defects. There can be neither honour nor reward in a service hidden, often enough, under the most utter incapacity and uselessness, as far as the world is concerned. Doubtless those who are given more important posts, are not, on this account, necessarily precluded from the state of abandonment. Less still is this state incompatible with striking virtue, and that sanctity which attracts universal veneration. Nevertheless there is a far greater number of souls raised to this sublime state whose virtue is known only to God. By their state these souls are free from nearly every outward obligation. They are little suited for worldly business or affairs, for complicated concerns, or for putting their mind into the conducting of industries. It seems as though they were quite useless; nothing is noticeable in them but feebleness of body, mind, imagination and passions. They take no notice of anything. They are, so to say, quite stupid, and possess nothing of that culture, study, or reflexion which go to the making of a man. They are like children of nature before they are placed in the hands of masters to be formed. They have noticeable faults which, without rendering them more guilty than children, cause more offence. God takes away everything but innocence in order that they should have nothing to rely upon but Him alone. The world, being in ignorance of this mystery can only judge by appearance, and can find nothing in them to its taste, nor anything that it values. It, therefore, rejects and despises them, and they seem to be exposed to censure from all. The more closely they are observed, the less is thought of them and the more opposition do they encounter; no one knows what to make of them. Although some hidden voice seems to speak in their favour, yet people prefer to adhere to their own malignant prepossessions rather than to follow this instinct, or at least to suspend their judgment. Their actions are pried into to find out their opinions, and like the Pharisees who could not endure the actions of Jesus, they are regarded with such prejudice that everything they do appears either ridiculous or criminal.

SECTION III.—*Self-Contempt.*

The third trial: interior humiliations.

Contemptible as they are in the eyes of others, the souls raised by God to this state are far more contemptible in their own. There is nothing either in what they do, or in what they suffer that is not altogether paltry and humiliating; there is nothing striking in anything about them, all is quite ordinary, nothing but troubles and afflictions interiorly, and contradictions and disappointments exteriorly. With a feeble body requiring many alleviations and comforts, the very reverse one would think of that spirit of poverty and austerity so much admired in the saints. Neither heroic undertakings, nor fasts, large alms, nor ardent and far-reaching zeal can be discerned in them; but united to God by faith and love they behold in themselves nothing but disorder. They despise themselves still more by comparison with those who pass for saints, and who, besides adapting themselves with facility to rules and methods show nothing irregular either in their persons or actions. Therefore their own short-comings in this respect fill them with confusion, and are unbearable to them. It is on this account that they give way to sighs and tears, marking the grief with which they are oppressed. Let us remember that Jesus Christ was both God and man; as man He was destroyed, and as God He remained full of glory. These souls have no participation in His glory, but they share in the sadness and misery of His sufferings. Men regard them in the same way as Herod and his court regarded Jesus Christ. These poor souls, therefore, are nourished as to their senses and mind, with a most disgusting food, in which they can find no pleasure. They aspire to something quite different, but all the avenues leading to the sanctity they so much desire, remain closed to them. They must live on this bread of suffering, on this bread mingled with ashes, with a continual shrinking both exterior and interior. They have formed an idea of saintliness which gives them constant and irremediable torment. The will hungers for it, but is powerless to practise it. Why should this be, except to mortify the soul in that which is its most spiritual and intimate part, which, finding no satisfaction or pleasure in anything that happens to it, must needs place all its affection in God who conducts it this way for the express purpose of preventing it taking pleasure in anything but Him alone.

It seems to me that it is easy to conclude from all this that souls abandoned to God cannot occupy themselves, as others do, with desires, examinations, cares, or attachments to certain persons. Neither can they form plans, nor lay down methodical rules for their actions, or for reading. This would imply that they still had power to dispose of themselves, which would entirely exclude the state of abandonment in which they are placed. In this state they give up to God all their rights over themselves, over their words, actions, thoughts, and proceedings; over the employment of their time and everything connected with it. There remains only one desire, to satisfy the Master they have chosen, to listen unceasingly to the expression of His will in order to execute it immediately. No condition can better represent this state than that of a servant who obeys every order he receives, and does not occupy his time in attending to his own affairs; these he neglects in order to serve His Master at every moment. These souls then should not be distressed at their powerlessness; they are able to do much in being able to give themselves entirely to a Master who is all-powerful, and able to work wonders with the feeblest of instruments if they offer no resistance.

Let us, then, endure without annoyance the humiliations entailed on us in our own eyes, and in the eyes of others, by what shows outwardly in our lives; or rather, let us conceal ourselves behind these outward appearances and enjoy God who is all ours. Let us profit by this apparent failure, by these requirements, by this care-taking and the necessity of constant nourishment, and of comfort; of our ill-success, of the contempt of others, of these fears, uncertainties, troubles, etc., to find all our wealth and happiness in God, who, by these means, gives Himself entirely to us as our only good. God wishes to be ours in a poor way, without all those accessories of sanctity which make others to be admired, and this is because God would have Himself to be the sole food of our souls, the only object of our desires. We are so weak that if we displayed the virtues of zeal, almsgiving, poverty, and austerity, we should make them subjects for vainglory. But as it is, everything is disagreeable in order that God may be our whole sanctification, our whole support, so that the world despises us, and leaves us to enjoy our treasure in peace. God desires to be the principle of all that is holy in us, and therefore what depends on ourselves and on our active fidelity is very small, and appears quite contrary to sanctity. There cannot be anything great in us in the sight of God except our passive endurance. Therefore let us think of it no more, let us leave the care of our sanctification to God who well knows how to effect it. It all depends on the watchful care, and particular operation of divine Providence, and is accomplished in a great measure without our knowledge, and even in a way that is unexpected, and disagreeable to us. Let us fulfil peacefully the little duties of our active fidelity, without aspiring to those that are greater, because God does not give Himself to us by reason of our own efforts. We shall become saints of God, of His grace, and of His special providence. He knows what rank to give us, let us leave it to Him, and without forming to ourselves false ideas, and empty systems of sanctity, let us content ourselves with loving Him unceasingly, and in pursuing with simplicity the path He has marked out for us, where all is so mean and paltry in our eyes, and in the estimation of the world.

SECTION IV.—*Distrust of Self.*

The fourth trial of souls in the state of abandonment: the obscurity of their state, and their apparent opposition to the will of God.

For a soul that desires nothing else but the will of God, what could be more miserable than the impossibility of being certain of loving Him? Formerly it was mentally enlightened to perceive in what consisted the plan for its perfection, but it is no longer able to do so in its present state. Perfection is given to it contrary to all preconceived ideas, to all light, to all feeling. It is given by all the crosses sent by Providence, by the action of present duties, by certain attractions, which have in them no good beyond that of not leading to sin; but seem very far from the dazzling sublimity of sanctity, and all that is unusual in virtue. God and His grace are given in a hidden and strange manner, for the soul feels too weak to bear the weight of its crosses, and disgusted with its obligations. Its attractions are only for quite ordinary exercises. The ideal it has formed of sanctity reproaches it interiorly for its mean and contemptible disposition. All books treating of the lives of the saints condemn it, it can find nothing in vindication of its conduct; it beholds a brilliant sanctity which renders it disconsolate because it has not strength sufficient to attain to it, and it does not see that its weakness is divinely ordered, but looks upon it as cowardice. Those whom it knows to be distinguished for striking virtue, of sublime contemplation regard it only with contempt. "What a strange saint," say they; and the soul, believing this, and confused by its countless useless efforts to raise itself from this low condition, is overwhelmed with opprobrium, and has nothing to advance in its own favour either to itself or to others. The soul in this state feels as if it were lost. Its reflexions afford it no help for its guidance, or enlightenment, and divine grace seems to have failed it. It is, however, through this loss that it finds again that same grace substituted under a different form, and restoring a hundredfold more than it took away by the purity of its hidden impressions.

This is, without doubt, a death-blow to the soul, for it loses sight of the divine will which, so to speak, withdraws itself from observation to stand behind it and push it on, becoming thus its invisible principle, and no longer its clearly defined object. Experience proves that nothing kindles the desire more than this apparent loss; therefore the soul vehemently desires to be united to the divine will, and gives vent to the most profound sighs, finding no possible consolation anywhere. A heart that has no other wish but to possess God must attract Him to itself, and this secret of love is a very great one since by this way alone are established in the soul sure faith and firm hope. It is then that we believe what we cannot see, and expect to possess what we cannot feel. Oh! how much does this incomprehensible conduct of an action, of which one is both subject and instrument, tend to one's perfection without any visible sign of appearance. Everything that one does seems done by chance, or natural inclination, and is very humiliating to the soul. When inspired to speak, it seems as if one spoke only from oneself. One never sees by what spirit one is impelled; the most divine inspiration is a terror, and whatever one does or feels is a source of constant self-contempt, as though it were all faulty and imperfect. Others are always admired, and one feels very inferior to them, while their whole way of acting causes confusion. The soul distrusts its own judgment, and cannot be certain about any of its thoughts; it pays excessive submission to the least advice given by a respectable authority, and the divine action in thus keeping it apart from striking virtue seems to plunge it into deeper humiliation. This humiliation has no appearance of virtue to the soul;

according to its own idea it is pure justice. The most admirable thing about it is, that in the eyes of others whom God does not enlighten, and even in its own eyes, the soul appears actuated by feelings absolutely contrary to virtue, such as pure obstinacy, disobedience, troublesomeness, contempt, and indignation, for which there seems no remedy. The more earnestly the soul strives to overcome these defects the more do they increase, because they form part of the design of God as being the most suitable means of detaching the soul from itself to prepare it for the divine union.

It is from this sad trial that the principal merit of the state of abandonment is gained. Now all is of a nature to withdraw the soul from its narrow path of love and simple obedience and it requires heroic virtue and courage to keep firm in plain active fidelity, and to sing its part in a song that seems to express in its tones that the soul is mistaken and lost; while grace sings a second. It does not hear this, however, and if it has courage to let the thunder roll, the lightning flash, and the tempest roar, and to walk with a firm tread in the path of love and obedience, of duty, and of the present attraction, it can be compared to the soul of Jesus during His passion, when our divine Saviour walked steadfastly in the fulfiling of the will of His Father, and in His love which imposed upon Him a task apparently quite inconsistent with the dignity of a soul of such sanctity as His.

The hearts of Jesus and Mary, bearing the fury of that darkest of nights, let the clouds gather, and the storm rage. A multitude of things in appearance most opposed to the designs of God and of His order, overwhelmed their faculties; but though deprived of all sensible support they walked without faltering in the path of love and obedience. Their eyes were fixed only on what they had to do, and leaving God to act as He pleased with all that concerned them, they endured the whole weight of that divine action. They groaned under the burden, but not for a single instant did they waver or pause. They believed that all would be well, provided that they kept on their way and let God act.

SECTION V.—*The Life of Faith.*

The fruit of these trials. The conduct of the submissive soul.

It results from all that has just been described that, in the path of pure faith, all that takes place spiritually, physically, and temporarily, has the aspect of death. This is not to be wondered at. What else could be expected? It is natural to this state. God has His plans for souls, and under this disguise He carries them out very successfully. Under the name of "disguise" I include ill-success, corporal infirmities, and spiritual weakness. All succeeds, and turns to good in the hands of God. It is by those things that are a trouble to nature that He prepares for the accomplishment of His greatest designs. "Omnia cooperantur in bonum iis qui secundum propositum vocati sunt sancti." "All things work together unto good to such as according to His purpose are called to be saints." (Rom. viii, 28). He brings life out of the shadow of death; therefore, when nature is afraid, faith, which takes everything in a good sense, is full of courage and confidence. To live by faith is to live by joy, confidence, and certainty about all that has to be done or suffered at each moment according to the designs of God. It is in order to animate and to maintain this life of faith that God allows the soul to be plunged into and carried away by the rough waters of so many pains, troubles, difficulties, fatigues and overthrows; for it requires faith to find God in all these things. The divine life is given at every moment in a hidden but very sure manner, under different appearances such as, the death of the body, the supposed loss of the soul, and the confusion of all earthly affairs. In all these, faith finds its food and support. It pierces through all, and clings to the hand of God, the giver of life. Through all that does not partake of the nature of sin, the faithful soul should proceed with confidence, taking it all as a veil, or disguise of God whose immediate presence alarms and at the same time reassures the faculties of the soul. In fact this great God who consoles the humble, gives the soul in the midst of its greatest desolation an interior assurance that it has nothing to fear, provided it allows Him to act, and abandons itself entirely to Him. It is grieved because it has lost its Well-beloved, and yet some-

thing assures it that it possesses Him. It is troubled and dis-
turbed, yet nevertheless has in its depths I know not what
important grounds for attaching itself steadfastly to God.
"Truly," said Jacob, "God is in this place, and I knew it not"
(Gen. xxviii, 16). You seek God and He is everywhere; everything proclaims Him, everything gives Him to you. He walks by
your side, is around you and within you: there He lives, and yet
you seek Him. You seek your own idea of God while all the time
you possess Him substantially. You seek perfection, and it is in
everything that presents itself to you. Your sufferings, your
actions, your attractions are the species under which God gives
Himself to you, while you are vainly striving after sublime ideas
which He by no means assumes in order to dwell in you.

Martha tried to please Jesus by cooking nice dishes, but Mary
was content to be with Jesus in any way that He wished to give
Himself to her; but when Mary sought Him in the garden
according to the idea she had formed of Him, He eluded her by
presenting Himself in the form of a gardener. The Apostles saw
Jesus, but mistook Him for a phantom. God disguises Himself,
therefore, to raise the soul to the state of pure faith, to teach it
to find Him under every kind of appearance; for, when it has
discovered this secret of God, it is in vain for Him to disguise
Himself; it says, "He is there, behind the wall, He is looking
through the lattice, looking from the windows" (Cant. ii, 9). Oh!
divine Love, hide yourself, proceed from one trial to another,
bind by attractions, blend, confuse, or break like threads all the
ideas and methods of the soul. May it stray hither and thither for
want of light, and be unable to see or understand in what path
it should walk; formerly it found You dwelling in Your ordinary
guise, in the peaceful repose of solitude and prayer, or in suffering; even in the consolations You give to others, in the course of
conversation, or in business; but now after having tried every
method known to please you, it has to stand aside not seeing
You in any of these things as in former times. May the uselessness of its efforts teach it to seek You henceforth in Yourself,
which means to seek You everywhere, in all things without distinction and without reflexion; for, oh divine Love! what a mistake it is, not to find you in all that is good, and in every creature.

Why then seek You in any other way than that by which You desire to give Yourself? Why, divine Love, seek You under any other species than those which You have chosen for Your Sacrament? The less there is to be seen or felt so much the more scope for faith and obedience. Do You not give fecundity to the root hidden underground, and can You not, if You so will, make this darkness in which You are pleased to keep me, fruitful? Live then, little root of my heart, in the deep, invisible heart of God; and by its power, send forth branches, leaves, flowers and fruits, which, although invisible to yourself, are a pure joy and nourishment to others. Without consulting your own taste, give of your shade, flowers, and fruit to others. May all that is grafted on you receive that indeterminate sap which will be known only by the growth and appearance of those same grafts. Become all to all, but as to yourself remain abandoned and indifferent. Remain in the dark and narrow prison of your miserable cocoon, little worm, until the warmth of grace forms you, and sets you free. Then feed upon whatever leaves it offers you, and do not regret, in the activity of abandonment, the peace you have lost. Stop directly the divine action would have you stop, and be content to lose, in the alternations of repose and activity, in incomprehensible changes, all your old formulas, methods and ways, to take upon you those designed for you by the divine action. Thus you will spin your silk in secret, doing what you can neither see nor feel. You will condemn in yourself a secret envy of your companions who are apparently dead and motionless, because they have not yet arrived at the point that you have attained; you continue to admire them although you have surpassed them. May your affliction in your abandonment continue while you spin a silk in which the princes of the Church and of the world and all sorts of souls will glory to be attired.

After that what will become of you, little worm? by what outlet will you come forth? Oh! marvel of grace by which souls are moulded in so many different shapes! Who can guess in what direction grace will guide it? And who could guess either, what nature does with a silkworm if he had not seen it working? It is only necessary to provide it with leaves, and nature does the rest.

Therefore no soul can tell from whence it came, nor whither it is going; neither from what thought of God the divine wisdom drew it, nor to what end it tends. Nothing is left but an entire passive abandonment, and to allow this divine Wisdom to act without interfering by our own reflexions, examples and methods. We must act when the time to act comes, and cease when it is time to stop; if necessary letting all be lost, and thus, acting or remaining passive according to attraction and abandonment we, insensibly, do, or leave undone without knowing what will be the result; and after many changes the formed soul receives wings and flies up to Heaven, leaving a plentiful harvest on earth for other souls to gather.

CHAPTER IV.

CONCERNING THE ASSISTANCE RENDERED
BY THE FATHERLY PROVIDENCE OF GOD TO THOSE SOULS
WHO HAVE ABANDONED THEMSELVES TO HIM.

SECTION I.—*Confidence in God.*

The less the soul in the state of abandonment feels the help it receives from God, the more efficaciously does He sustain it.

There is a kind of sanctity in which all the communications of God are luminous and distinct; but in the passive state of pure faith all that God communicates partakes of the nature of that inaccessible darkness that surrounds His throne, and all ideas are confused and indistinct. The soul, in this state of obscurity is often afraid, like the Prophet, of running headlong against a rock. "Fear not, faithful soul, for this is your right path, and the way by which God conducts you. There is no way more safe and sure than this dark way of faith." "But it is so dark that I cannot tell which way to go." "Go wherever you please; you cannot lose the way where there is no path; every way looks the same in the dark, you cannot see the end because nothing is visible." "But I am afraid of everything. I feel as if, at any moment, I might fall over a precipice. Everything is an affliction to me; I well know that I am acting according to abandonment, but it seems to me that there are things I cannot do without acting contrary to virtue. I seem to be so far from all the virtues. The more I wish to practise them the more remote they seem. I love virtue, but the obscure impressions by which I am attracted seem to keep virtue far from me. I always give in to this attraction, and although I cannot perceive that it guides me well, I cannot help following it. The spirit seeks light; but the heart is in darkness. Enlightened persons, and those with lucid minds are congenial to my spirit, but when I hear conversations and listen to discourses, my heart understands nothing; its whole state and way is simply an impression of the gift of faith, which makes it love and appreciate those principles, truths, and paths wherein the spirit has neither object nor idea, and in which it trembles, shudders, and falters. I have an assurance, I do not know how, in the depths of my heart, that this way is right; not by the evidence of my senses, but by a feeling inspired by faith." This is because it is impossible for God to lead a soul without persuading it that the path is a right one, and this with a certainty all the greater the less it is perceived. And this certainty is victorious over all censures, fears, efforts, and all imaginations. The mind vainly cries out and seeks some better way. The bride recognises the Bridegroom unconsciously, but when she stretches out her hand to hold Him, He disappears. She understands that the Spouse to whom she belongs has rights over her, and she prefers to wander without order or method in abandoning herself to His guidance rather than to endeavour to gain confidence by following the beaten tracks of virtue.

Let us go to God, then, my soul, in abandonment, and let us acknowledge that we are incapable of acquiring virtue by our own industry or effort; but let us not allow this absence of particular virtues to diminish our confidence. Our divine Guide would not have reduced us to the necessity of walking if He had not intended to carry us in His arms. What need have we of lights and certainties, ideas and reflexions? Of what use would it be to us to see, to know, and to feel, when we are no longer walking but being carried in the arms of divine Providence. The more we have to suffer from darkness, and the more rocks, precipices, and deserts there are in our way; the more we have to endure from fears, dryness, weariness of mind, anguish of soul, and even despair, and the sight of purgatory and hell, the greater must be our confidence and faith. One glance at Him who carries us is sufficient to restore our courage in the greatest peril. We will forget the paths and what they are like; we will forget ourselves, and abandoning ourselves entirely to the wisdom, goodness, and power of our Guide we will think only of loving Him, and avoiding all sin, not only that which is evident, however venial it may be, but even the appearance of evil, and of fulfilling all the duties and obligations of our state.

This is the only charge You lay upon Your children, O divine Love! all the rest You take upon Yourself. The more terrible this may be, the more surely can Your presence be felt and recognised. Your children have only to love You without ceasing, and to fulfil their small duties like children. A child on its mother's lap is occupied only with its games as if it had nothing else to do but to play with its mother. The soul should soar above the clouds, and, as no one can work during the darkness of the night, it is the time for repose. The light of reason can do nothing but deepen the darkness of faith: the radiance necessary to disperse it must proceed from the same source as itself. In this state God communicates Himself to the soul as its life, but He is no longer visible as its way, and its truth: The bride seeks the Bridegroom during this night; she seeks Him before her, and hurries forward; but He is behind her, and holding her with His hands. He is no longer object, or idea, but principle and source. For all the needs, difficulties, troubles, falls, overthrows, persecutions, and uncertainties of souls which have lost all confidence in themselves and their own action, there are secret and inspired resources in the divine action, marvellous and unknown. The more perplexing the circumstances the keener is the expectation of a satisfactory solution. The heart says "All goes well, it is God who carries on the work, there is nothing to fear." That very suspense and desolation are verses in the canticle of darkness. It is a joy that not a single syllable is left out, and it all ends in a "Gloria Patri"; therefore we pursue the way of our wanderings, and darkness itself is a light for our guidance; and doubts are our best assurance. The more puzzled Isaac was to find something to sacrifice, the more completely did Abraham place all in the hands of Providence, and trust entirely in God.

SECTION II.—*Diversity of Grace.*

The afflictions which the soul is made to endure are but loving artifices of God which will, one day, give it great joy.

Souls that walk in light sing the canticles of the light; those that walk in darkness sing the songs of the darkness. Both must be allowed to sing to the end the part allotted to them by God in the great Oratorio. Nothing must be added to the score, nothing left out; every drop of bitterness must be allowed to flow freely at whatever cost. It was thus with Jeremias and Ezechiel whose utterances were broken by tears and sobs, and who could find no consolation except in continuing their lamentations. Had the course of their grief been interrupted, we should have lost the most beautiful passages of Scripture. The Spirit that afflicts can also console; these diverse waters flow from the same source. When God appears angry the soul trembles; when He threatens it is terrified. The divine operation must be allowed to develop, for, with the evil it carries a remedy; so continue to weep and to tremble; let restlessness and agony invade your souls, make no effort to free yourselves from these divine terrors, these heavenly troubles, but open your hearts to receive these little streams from that immense sea of sorrows which God bore in His most holy soul. Sow in sorrow for as long as grace requires, and that same grace will gradually dry your tears. Darkness will disappear before the radiance of the sun, springtime will come with its flowers, and the result of your abandonment will be seen in the admirable diversity of the divine action. Indeed it is quite useless for man to trouble himself; all that takes place in him is like a dream. One cloud chases another like imaginations in the brain of the sleeper, some sorrowful, others consoling. The soul is the playground of these phantoms which follow each other with great rapidity, and on awaking it feels that, in all this, there is nothing to detain it. When these impressions have passed away it takes no notice of the joys or sorrows of dreams.

O Lord! it can be truly said that You carry Your children in Your arms during this long night of faith, and that You are pleased to allow an infinite variety of thoughts to pass through their minds; thoughts holy and mysterious. In the state in which these dreams of the night place them, they indeed experience the utmost torment of fear, anguish, and weariness, but on the bright day of eternal glory these will give place to a true and solid joy.

It is at the moment of, and just after the awakening that holy souls, returning to themselves, and with full right to judge, can never tire of admiring and praising the tact, the inventions and refinements of loving deception practised by the divine Spouse. They understand how impenetrable are His ways, how impossible it is to guess His enigmas, to find out His disguises, or to receive consolation when it is His will to spread terror and alarm.

At this awakening those who, like Jeremias and David, have been inconsolable in their grief, will see that in their desolation they have been a subject of joy to the angels, and of glory to God. The bride sleeps through the bustle of industries, and of human actions, and in spite of the sneers of sceptics. In her sleep she will sigh and tremble; in her dreams she will pursue and seek her Spouse, who disguises Himself to deceive her.

Let her dream; her fears are only born of the night, and of sleep. When the Spouse has exercised her beloved soul, and shown forth in it what can only be expressed by Him, He will develop the result of these dreams and will awaken it at the right time.

Joseph caused Benjamin to weep, and his servants kept his secret from this beloved brother. Joseph deceived him, and not all his penetration and wit could fathom this deception. Benjamin and his brothers were plunged in unspeakable sorrow but Joseph was only playing a trick on them, although the poor brothers could see nothing but an evil without any remedy. When he reveals himself and puts everything right they admire his wisdom in making them think that all is lost, and to cause them to despair about that which turns out to be a subject of the greatest joy they have ever experienced.

SECTION III.—*The Generosity of God.*

The more God seems to despoil the soul that is in the state of abandonment, the more generous are His gifts.

Let us continue to advance in the knowledge of the divine action and of its loving deceptions. That which it withdraws from the perception, it bestows incognito, as it were, on the goodwill. It never allows it to want for anything. It is as if someone who had maintained a friend by bounties bestowed personally upon him, should suddenly, for the welfare of this same friend, pretend that he could no longer oblige him, yet continues to assist him without making himself known. The friend, not suspecting any stratagem in this mystery of love, feels hurt, and entertains all sorts of ideas and criticisms on the conduct of his benefactor.

When, however, the mystery begins to be revealed, God knows what different feelings arise in the soul; joy, tenderness, gratitude, love, confusion and admiration; followed by an increase of zeal for, and attachment to the benefactor. And this trial will be the means of strengthening the soul, and accustoming it to similar surprises.

The application is easy. With God, the more one seems to lose the more one gains. The more He strikes off of what is natural, the more He gives of what is supernatural. He is loved at first for His gifts, but when these are no longer perceptible He is at last loved for Himself. It is by the apparent withdrawal of these sensible gifts that He prepares the way for that great gift which is the most precious and the most extensive of all, since it embraces all others. Souls which have once for all submitted themselves to the divine action, ought to interpret everything favourably. Yes, everything! even the loss of the most excellent directors, and the want of confidence they cannot help feeling in those who offer themselves for that post.

In truth those guides who, of their own accord, run after souls, deserve to be distrusted. Those who are truly inspired by the spirit of God do not, as a rule, show so much eagerness and self-sufficiency. They do not come forward until they are appealed to, and even then they proceed with caution. May the soul that has given itself entirely to God pass without fear through all these trials without losing its balance. Provided it is faithful to the divine action, this all-powerful action can produce marvels in it in spite of every obstacle.

God and the soul work in common, and the success of the work depends entirely on the divine Workman, and can only be spoilt if the soul prove unfaithful. When the soul is well, all is well, because what is from God, that is to say, His part and His action are, as it were, the counterpoise of the fidelity of the soul. It is the best part of the work, which is done something like beautiful tapestry, stitch by stitch from the wrong side. The worker employed on it sees only the stitch he is making, and the needle with which he makes it, while all the stitches combined form magnificent figures which do not show until, every part being complete, the right side is turned outwards. All the beauty and perfection of the work remain in obscurity during its progress. It is the same with the soul that has abandoned itself to God; it has eyes only for Him and for its duty. The performance of this duty is, at each moment, but an imperceptible stitch added to the work, and yet with these stitches God performs wonders of which He sometimes allows a glimpse to be seen, but which will not be visible in their entirety till revealed on the great day of eternity. How full of goodness and wisdom is the guidance of God! He has so entirely kept for His own grace, and His own action, all that is admirable, great, exalted and sublime; and so completely left to our souls, with the aid of grace, all that is little, light and easy, that there is no one in the world who cannot easily reach a most eminent degree of perfection in accomplishing lovingly the most ordinary and obscure duties.

SECTION IV.—*The Most Ordinary Things are Channels of Grace.*

In the state of abandonment God guides the soul more safely the more completely He seems to blind it.

It is most especially with regard to souls that abandon themselves entirely to God that the words of St. John are applicable: "You have no need that any man teach you, as His unction teacheth you of all things" (I Eph., St. John, ii, 20). To know what God demands of them they need only probe their own hearts, and listen to the inspirations of this unction, which interpret the will of God according to circumstances.

The divine action, concealed though it is, reveals its designs, not through ideas, but intuitively. It shows them to the soul either necessarily, by not permitting any other thing to be chosen but what is actually present, or else by a sudden impulse, a sort of supernatural feeling that impels the soul to act without premeditation; or, in fine, by some kind of inclination or aversion which, while leaving it complete liberty, yet none the less leads it to take or refuse what is presented to it. If one were to judge by appearances, it seems as if it would be a great want of virtue to be swayed and influenced in this manner; and if one were to judge by ordinary rules, there appears a want of regulation and method in such conduct; but in reality it is the highest degree of virtue, and only after having practised it for a long time does one succeed. The virtue in this state is pure virtue; it is, in fact, perfection itself. One is like a musician, who combines a perfect knowledge of music with technical skill: he would be so full of his art that, without thinking, all that he performed within its compass would be perfect; and if his compositions were examined afterwards, they would be found in perfect conformity with prescribed rules. One would then become convinced that he would never succeed better than when, free from the rules that keep genius in fetters when too scrupulously followed, he acted without constraint; and that his impromptus would be admired as chef d'œuvres by all connoisseurs. Thus the soul, trained for a long time in the science and practice of perfection under the influence of reasonings and methods of which it made use to assist grace, forms for itself a habit of acting in all things by the instincts implanted by God. It then knows that it can do nothing better than what first presents itself, without all those arguments of which it had need formerly. The only thing to be done is to act at random when unable to trust in anything but the workings of grace which cannot mislead it. The effects of grace, visible to watchful eyes, and intelligent minds, are nothing short of marvellous.

Without method, yet most exact; without rule, yet most orderly; without reflexion, yet most profound; without skill, yet thoroughly well constructed; without effort, yet everything accomplished; and without foresight, yet nothing better suited to unexpected events. Spiritual reading with the divine action, often contains a meaning that the author never thought of. God makes use of the words and actions of others to infuse truths which might otherwise have remained hidden. If He wishes to impart light in this way, it is for the submissive soul to avail itself of this light. Every expedient of the divine action has an efficacy which always surpasses its apparent and natural virtue.

It is the nature of abandonment always to lead a mysterious life, and to receive great and miraculous gifts from God by means of the most ordinary things, things that may be natural, accidental, or that seem to happen by chance, and in which there seems no other agency than the ordinary course of the ways of the world, or of the elements. In this way the simplest sermons, the most commonplace conversations, and the least high-toned books, become to these souls, by the virtue of God's will, sources of knowledge and wisdom. This is why they carefully gather up the crumbs that sceptics trample underfoot. Everything is precious in their eyes, everything enriches them. They are inexpressibly indifferent towards all things, and yet neglect nothing, having a respect for, and making use of all things. As God is everywhere, the use made of things by His will is not so much the use of creatures, as the enjoyment of the divine action which transmits His gifts by different channels. They cannot sanctify of themselves, but only as instruments of the divine action, which has power to communicate His grace, and often does communicate it to simple souls in ways and by means which seem opposed to the end intended. It enlightens through mud as well as through glass, and the instrument of which it makes use is always singular. To it everything is alike. Faith always believes that nothing is wanting to it, and never complains of the privation of means which might prove useful for its increase, because the Workman, who employs them efficaciously, supplies what is wanting by His action. The divine action is the whole virtue of the creature.

SECTION V.—*Nature and Grace the Instruments of God.*

The less capable the soul in the state of abandonment is of defending itself, the more powerfully does God defend it.

The one and infallible influence of the divine action is invariably applied to the submissive soul at an opportune moment, and this soul corresponds in everything to its interior direction. It is pleased with everything that has taken place, with everything that is happening, and with all that affects it, with the exception of sin. Sometimes the soul acts with full consciousness, sometimes unknowingly, being led only by obscure instincts to say, to do, or to leave certain things, without being able to give a reason for its action.

Often the occasion and the determining reason are only of the natural order; the soul, perceiving no sort of mystery therein, acts by pure chance, necessity, or convenience, and its act has no other aspect either in its own eyes, or those of others; while all the time the divine action, through the intellect, the wisdom, or the counsel of friends, makes use of the simplest things in its favour. It makes them its own, and opposes so persistently every effort prejudicial to them, that it becomes impossible that these should succeed.

To have to deal with a simple soul is, in a certain way, to have to deal with God. What can be done against the will of the Almighty and His inscrutable designs? God takes the cause of the simple soul in hand. It is unnecessary for it to study the intrigues of others, to trouble about their worries, or to scrutinize their conduct; its Spouse relieves it of all these anxieties, and it can repose in Him full of peace, and in security.

The divine action frees and exempts the soul from all those low and noisy ways so necessary to human prudence. These suited Herod and the Pharisees, but the Magi had only to follow their star in peace. The child has but to rest in His Mother's arms. His enemies do more to advance His interests than to hinder His work. The greater efforts they exert to thwart, and to take Him unawares, the more freely and tranquilly does He act. He never humours them, nor basely truckles to them to make them turn aside their blows; their jealousies, suspicions, and persecutions are necessary to Him. Thus did Jesus Christ live in Judea, and thus does He live now in simple souls. In them He is generous, sweet, free, peaceful, fearless, needing no one, beholding all creatures in His Father's hands, and obliged to serve Him, some by their criminal passions, others by their holy actions; the former by their contradictions, the latter by their obedience and submission. The divine action balances all this in a wonderful manner, nothing is wanting nor is anything superfluous, but of good and evil there is only what is necessary. The will of God applies, at each moment, the proper means to the end in view, and the simple soul, instructed by faith, finds everything right, and desires neither more nor less than what it has. It ever blesses that divine hand which so well apportions the means, and turns every obstacle aside. It receives friends and enemies with the same patient courtesy with which Jesus treated everyone, and as divine instruments. It has need of no one and yet needs all. The divine action renders all necessary, and all must be received from it, according to their quality and nature, and corresponded to with sweetness and humility; the simple treated simply, and the unpolished kindly. This is what St Paul teaches, and what Jesus Christ practised most perfectly.

Only grace can impress this supernatural character, which is appropriate to, and adapts itself to each person. This is never learnt from books, but from a true prophetic spirit, and is the effect of a special inspiration, and a doctrine of the Holy Spirit. To understand it one must be in the highest state of abandonment, the most perfect freedom from all design, and from all interests, however holy. One must have in view the only serious business in the world, that of following submissively the divine action. To do this one must apply oneself to the fulfilling of the obligations of one's state; and allow the Holy Spirit to act interiorly without trying to understand His operations, but even being pleased to be kept in ignorance about them. Then one is safe, for all that happens in the world can work nothing but good for souls perfectly submissive to the will of God.

SECTION VI.—*Supernatural Prudence.*

The soul, in the state of abandonment, does not fear its enemies, but finds in them useful helps.

I fear more my own action and that of my friends than that of
my enemies. There is no prudence so great as that which offers
no resistance to enemies, and which opposes to them only a
simple abandonment. This is to run before the wind, and as
there is nothing else to be done, to keep quiet and peaceful.
There is nothing that is more entirely opposed to worldly prudence than simplicity; it turns aside all schemes without comprehending them, without so much as a thought about them.
The divine action makes the soul take such just measures as to
surprise those who want to take it by surprise themselves. It
profits by all their efforts, and is raised by the very things that
are done to lower it. They are the galley slaves who bring the
ship into port with hard rowing. All obstacles turn to the good
of this soul, and by allowing its enemies a free hand, it obtains a
continual service, so sufficing that all it has to fear is lest it
should itself take part in a work of which God would be principal, and His enemies the agents, and in which it has nothing to
do but to peacefully observe the work of God, and to follow with
simplicity the attractions He gives it. The supernatural prudence of the Divine Spirit, the principle of these attractions,
infallibly attains its end; and the precise circumstances of each
event are so applied to the soul, without its perception, that
everything opposed to them cannot fail to be destroyed.

SECTION VII.—*Conviction of Weakness.*

The soul in the state of abandonment can abstain from justify-
ing itself by word or deed. The divine action justifies it.

This order of the divine will is the solid and firm rock on
which the submissive soul reposes, sheltered from change and
tempest. It is continually present under the veil of crosses, and
of the most ordinary actions. Behind this veil the hand of God is
hidden to sustain and to support those who abandon themselves

entirely to Him. From the time that a soul becomes firmly
established in abandonment, it will be protected from the opposition of talkers, for it need not ever say or do anything in self-
defence. Since the work is of God, justification must never be
sought elsewhere. Its effects and its consequences are justification enough. There is nothing but to let it develop "Dies diei
eructat verbum"; "Day to day uttereth speech" (Ps. xviii, 3).
When one is no longer guided by reflexion, words must no longer be used in self-defence. Our words can only express our
thoughts; where no ideas are supposed to exist, words cannot be
used. Of what use would they be? To give a satisfactory explana-
tion of our conduct? But we cannot explain that of which we
know nothing for it is hidden in the principle of our actions, and
we have experienced nothing but an impression, and that in an
ineffable manner. We must, therefore, let the results justify
their principles.

All the links of this divine chain remain firm and solid, and
the reason of that which precedes as cause is seen in that
which follows as effect. It is no longer a life of dreams, a life of
imaginations, a life of a multiplicity of words. The soul is no
longer occupied with these things, nor nourished and maintained in this way; they are no longer of any avail, and afford
no support.

The soul no longer sees where it is going, nor foresees where
it will go; reflexions no longer help it to gain courage to endure
fatigue, and to sustain the hardships of the way. All this is swept
aside by an interior conviction of weakness. The road widens as
it advances; it has started, and goes on without hesitation. Being
perfectly simple and straightforward, it follows the path of God's
commandments quietly, relying on God Himself whom it finds
at every step, and God, whom it seeks above all things, takes
upon Himself to manifest His presence in such a way as to
avenge it on its unjust detractors.

SECTION VIII.—*Self-guidance a Mistake.*

God imparts to the soul in the state of abandonment by
means which seem more likely to destroy it.

There is a time when God would be the life of the soul, and Himself accomplish its perfection in secret and unknown ways. Then all its own ideas, lights, industries, examinations, and reasonings become sources of illusion. After many experiences of the sad consequences of self-guidance, the soul recognising its uselessness, and finding that God has hidden and confused all the issues, is forced to fly to Him to find life. Then, convinced of its nothingness and of the harmfulness of all that it derives from itself, it abandons itself to God to gain all from Him. It is then that God becomes the source of its life, not by means of ideas, lights, or reflexions, for all this is no longer anything to it but a source of illusion; but in reality, and by His grace, which is hidden under the strangest appearances.

The divine operation, unknown to the soul, communicates its virtue and substance by many circumstances that the soul believes will be its destruction. There is no cure for this ignorance, it must be allowed its course. God gives Himself therein, and with Himself, he gives all things in the obscurity of faith. The soul is but a blind subject, or, in other words, it is like a sick person who knows nothing of the properties of remedies and tastes only their bitterness. He often imagines that what is given him will be his death; the pain and weakness which result seem to justify his fears; nevertheless it is under the semblance of death that his health is restored, and he takes the medicines on the word of the physician. In the same way the submissive soul is in no way pre-occupied about its infirmities, except as regards obvious maladies which by their nature compel it to rest, and to take suitable remedies. The languor and weakness of souls in the state of abandonment are only illusory appearances which they ought to defy with confidence. God sends them, or permits them in order to give opportunities for the exercise of faith and abandonment which are the true remedies. Without paying the least attention to them, these souls should generously pursue their way, following by their actions and sufferings the order of God, making use without hesitation of the body as though it were a horse on hire, which is intended to be driven until it is worn out. This is better than thinking of health so much as to harm the soul.

A courageous spirit does much to maintain a feeble body, and one year of a life spent in so noble and generous a manner is of more value than would be a century of care-taking and nervous fears. One ought to be able to show outwardly that one is in a state of grace and goodwill. What is there to be afraid of in fulfilling the divine will? The conduct of one who is upheld and sustained by it should show nothing exteriorly but what is heroic. The terrifying experiences that have to be encountered are really nothing. They are only sent that life may be adorned with more glorious victories. The divine will involves the soul in troubles of every kind, where human prudence can neither see nor imagine any outlet. It then feels all its weakness, and, finding out its shortcomings, is confounded. The divine will then asserts itself in all its power to those who give themselves to it without reserve. It succours them more marvellously than the writers of fiction, in the fertility of their imagination, unravel the intrigues and perils of their imaginary heroes, and bring them to a happy end. With a much more admirable skill, and much more happily, does the divine will guide the soul through deadly perils and monsters, even through the fires of hell with their demons and sufferings. It raises souls to the heights of heaven, and makes them the subjects of histories both real and mystical, more beautiful, and more extraordinary than any invented by the vain imagination of man.

On then, my soul, through perils and monsters, guided and sustained by that mighty invisible hand of divine Providence. On, without fear, to the end, in peace and joy, and make all the incidents of life occasions of fresh victories. We march under His Standard, to fight and to conquer; "exivit vincens ut vinceret"; "He went forth conquering that he might conquer" (Apocal. vi, 2).

As many steps as we take under His command will be the triumphs we gain. The Holy Spirit of God writes in an open book this sacred history which is not yet finished, nor will be till the end of the world. This history contains an account of the guidance and designs of God with regard to men. It remains for us to figure in this history, and to continue the thread of it by the union of our actions and sufferings with His will. No! It is not to cause the loss of our souls that we have so much to do, and to suffer; but that we may furnish matter for that holy writing which is added to day by day.

SECTION IX.—*Divine Love, the Principle of All Good.*

To those who follow this path, divine love is all-sufficing.

While despoiling of all things those souls who give themselves entirely to Him, God gives them something in place of them. Instead of light, wisdom, life, and strength, He gives them His love. The divine love in these souls is like a supernatural instinct. In nature, each thing contains that which is suitable to its kind. Each flower has its special beauty, each animal its instinct, and each creature its perfection. Also in the different states of grace, each has a special grace. This is the recompense for everyone who accepts with goodwill the state in which he is placed by Providence. A soul comes under the divine action from the moment that a habit of goodwill is formed within it, and this action influences it more or less according to its degree of abandonment. The whole art of abandonment is simply that of loving, and the divine action is nothing else than the action of divine love. How can it be that these two loves seeking each other should do otherwise than unite when they meet? How can the divine love refuse aught to a soul whose every desire it directs? And how can a soul that lives only for Him refuse Him anything? Love can refuse nothing that love desires, nor desire anything that love refuses. The divine action regards only the goodwill; the capability of the other faculties does not attract it, nor does the want of capability repel it. All that it requires is a heart that is good, pure, just, simple, submissive, filial, and respectful. It takes possession of such a heart, and of all its faculties, and so arranges everything for its benefit that it finds in all things its sanctification. That which destroys other souls would find in this soul an antidote of goodwill which would nullify its poison. Even at the edge of a precipice the divine action would draw it back, or even if it were allowed to remain there it would prevent it from falling; and if it fell, it would rescue it. After all, the faults of such a soul are only faults of frailty; love takes but little notice of them, and well knows how to turn them to advantage. It makes the soul understand by secret suggestions what it ought to say, or to do, according to circumstances. These suggestions it receives as rays of light from the divine understanding: "intellectus bonus omnibus facientibus eum"; "A good understanding to all that do it" (Ps. cx, 10), for this divine understanding accompanies such souls step by step, and prevents them taking those false steps which their simplicity encourages. If they make arrangements which would involve them in some promise prejudicial to them, divine Providence arranges some fortunate occurrence which rectifies everything. In vain are schemes formed against them repeatedly; divine Providence cuts all the knots, brings the authors to confusion, and so turns their heads as to make them fall into their own trap. Under its guidance those souls that they wish to take by surprise do certain things that seem very useless at the time, but that serve afterwards to deliver them from all the troubles into which their uprightness and the malice of their enemies would have plunged them. Oh! what good policy it is to have goodwill! What prudence there is in simplicity! What ability in its innocence and candour! What mysteries and secrets in its straightforwardness! Look at the youthful Tobias; he is but a lad, yet with what confidence he proceeds, having the archangel Raphael for his guide. Nothing frightens him, nothing is wanting to him. The very monsters he encounters furnish him with food and remedies; the one that rushes forward to devour him becomes itself his sustenance. By the order of Providence he has nothing to attend to but feasts and weddings, everything else is left to the management of the guiding spirit appointed to help him. These things are so well managed that never before have they been so successful, nor so blessed and prosperous. However, his mother weeps, and is in great distress at his supposed loss, but his father remains full of faith. The son, so bitterly mourned, returns to rejoice his family and to share their happiness.

Divine love then, is to those who give themselves up to it without reserve, the principle of all good. To acquire this inestimable treasure the only thing necessary is greatly to desire it.

Yes, God only asks for love, and if you seek this treasure, this kingdom in which God reigns alone, you will find it. If your heart is entirely devoted to God, it is itself, for that very reason, the treasure and the kingdom that you seek and desire. From the time that one desires God and His holy will, one enjoys God and His will, and this enjoyment corresponds to the ardour of the desire. To desire to love God is truly to love Him, and because we love Him we wish to become instruments of His action in order that His love may be exercised in, and by us. The divine action does not correspond to the aims of a saintly and simple soul, nor to the steps it takes, nor to the projects it forms, nor to the manner in which it reflects, nor to the means it chooses, nor to the purity of its intention. It often happens that the soul can be deceived in all this, but its good intention and uprightness can never deceive it. Provided that God perceives in it a good intention, He can dispense with all the rest, and He holds as done for Him what it will eventually do when truer ideas second its goodwill.

Goodwill, therefore, has nothing to fear. If it fall, it can only do so under the almighty hand which guides and sustains it in all its wanderings. It is this divine hand which turns it again to face the goal from which it has strayed; which replaces it in the right path when it has wandered. In it the soul finds resources for the deviations to which the blind faculties which deceive it, render it subject. It is made to feel how much it ought to despise them, and to rely on God alone, abandoning itself absolutely to His infallible guidance. The failings into which good souls fall are put an end to by abandonment. Never can goodwill be taken unawares. That all things work for its good is an article of faith.

SECTION X.—*We Must see God in all His Creatures.*

In the state of abandonment the soul finds more light and strength, through submission to the divine action, than all those possess who resist it through pride.

Of what use are the most sublime illuminations, the most divine revelations, if one has no love for the will of God? It was because of this that Lucifer fell. The ruling of the divine action revealed to him by God, in showing him the mystery of the Incarnation, produced in him nothing but envy.

On the other hand a simple soul, enlightened only by faith, can never tire of admiring, praising, and loving the order of God; of finding it not only in holy creatures, but even in the most irregular confusion and disorder. One grain of pure faith will give more light to a simple soul than Lucifer received in his highest intelligence. The devotion of the faithful soul to its obligations; its quiet submission to the intimate promptings of grace; its gentleness and humility towards everyone; are of more value than the most profound insight into mysteries. If one regarded only the divine action in all the pride and harshness of creatures, one would never treat them with anything but sweetness and respect. Their roughness would never disturb the divine order, whatever course it might take. One must only see in it the divine action, given and taken, as long as one is faithful in the practice of sweetness and humility. It is best not to observe their way of proceeding, but always to walk with firm steps in our own path. It is thus that by bending gently, cedars are broken, and rocks overthrown. Who amongst creatures can resist a faithful, gentle, and humble soul? These are the only arms to be taken if we wish to conquer all our enemies. Jesus Christ has placed them in our hands that we may defend ourselves; there is nothing to fear if we know how to use them.

We must not be cowardly, but generous. This is the only disposition suitable to the instruments of God.

All the works of God are sublime and marvellous; while one's own actions, when they war against God, cannot resist the divine action in one who is united to it by sweetness and humility.

Who is Lucifer? He is a pure spirit, and was the most enlightened of all pure spirits, but is now at war with God and with His rule. The mystery of sin is merely the result of this conflict, which manifests itself in every possible way. Lucifer, as much as in him lies, will leave no stone upturned to destroy what God has made and ordered. Wherever he enters, there is the work of God defaced. The more light, science, and capacity a person has, the more he is to be feared if he does not possess a foundation of piety, which consists in being satisfied with God and His will. It is by a well-regulated heart that one is united to the divine action; without this everything is purely natural, and generally, in direct opposition to the divine order. God makes use only of the humble as His instruments. Always contradicted by the proud, He yet makes use of them, like slaves, for the accomplishment of His designs.

When I find a soul which does all for God alone, and in submission to His order, however wanting it may be in all things else, I say "This is a soul with a great aptitude for serving God." The holy Virgin and St. Joseph were like this. All else without these qualities makes me fear. I am afraid to see in it the action of Lucifer. I remain on my guard, and shut myself up in my foundation of simplicity, in opposition to all this outward glitter which, by itself, is nothing to me but a bit of broken glass.

SECTION XI.—*The Strength of Simplicity*.

The soul in the state of abandonment knows how to see God even in the proud who oppose His action. All creatures, good or evil, reveal Him to it.

The whole practice of the simple soul is in the accomplishment of the will of God. This it respects even in those unruly actions by which the proud attempt to depreciate it. The proud soul despises one in whose sight it is as nothing, who beholds only God in it, and in all its actions. Often it imagines that the modesty of the simple soul is a mark of appreciation for itself; when, all the time, it is only a sign of that loving fear of God and of His holy will as shown to it in the person of the proud. No, poor fool, the simple soul fears you not at all. You excite its compassion; it is answering God when you think it is speaking to you: it is with Him that it believes it has to do; it regards you only as one of His slaves, or rather as a mask with which He disguises Himself. Therefore the more you take a high tone, the lower you become in its estimation; and when you think to take it by surprise, it surprises you. Your wiles and violence are just favours from Heaven.

The proud soul cannot comprehend itself, but the simple soul, with the light of faith, can very clearly see through it.

The finding of the divine action in all that occurs at each moment, in and around us, is true science, a continuous revelation of truth, and an unceasingly renewed intercourse with God. It is a rejoicing with the Spouse, not in secret, nor by stealth, in the cellar, or the vineyard, but openly, and in public, without any human respect. It is a fund of peace, of joy, of love, and of satisfaction with God who is seen, known, or rather, believed in, living and operating in the most perfect manner in everything that happens. It is the beginning of eternal happiness not yet perfectly realised and tasted, except in an incomplete and hidden manner.

The Holy Spirit, who arranges all the pieces on the board of life, will, by this fruitful and continual presence of His action, say at the hour of death, "fiat lux," "let there be light" (Gen. i, 14), and then will be seen the treasures which faith hides in this abyss of peace and contentment with God, and which will be found in those things that have been every moment done, or suffered for Him.

When God gives Himself thus, all that is common becomes wonderful; and it is on this account that nothing seems to be so, because this way is, in itself, extraordinary. Consequently it is unnecessary to make it full of strange and unsuitable marvels. It is, in itself, a miracle, a revelation, a constant joy even with the prevalence of minor faults. But it is a miracle which, while rendering all common and sensible things wonderful, has nothing in itself that is sensibly marvellous.

SECTION XII.—*The Triumph of Humility.*

To the souls which are faithful to Him, God promises a glorious victory over the powers of the world and of hell.

If the divine action is hidden here below under the appearance of weakness, it is in order to increase the merit of souls which are faithful to it; but its triumph is none the less certain.

The history of the world from the beginning is but the history of the struggle between the powers of the world, and of hell, against the souls which are humbly devoted to the divine action. In this struggle all the advantage seems to be on the side of pride, yet the victory always remains with humility. The image of the world is always presented to our eyes as a statue of gold, brass, iron, and clay. This mystery of iniquity, shown in a dream to Nabuchodonosor, is nothing but a confused medley of all the actions, interior and exterior, of the children of darkness. This is also typified by the beast coming out of the pit to make war, from the beginning of time, against the interior and spiritual life of man. All that takes place in our days is the consequence of this war. Monster follows monster out of the pit, which swallows, and vomits them forth again amidst incessant clouds of smoke. The combat between St. Michael and Lucifer, that began in Heaven, still continues. The heart of this once magnificent angel, has become, through envy, an inexhaustible abyss of every kind of evil. He made angel revolt against angel in Heaven, and from the creation of the world his whole energy is exerted to make more criminals among men to fill the ranks of those who have been swallowed up in the pit. Lucifer is the chief of those who refuse obedience to the Almighty. This mystery of iniquity is the very inversion of the order of God; it is the order, or rather, the disorder of the devil.

This disorder is a mystery because, under a false appearance of good, it hides irremediable and infinite evil. Every wicked man, who, from the time of Cain, up to the present moment, has declared war against God, has outwardly been great and powerful, making a great stir in the world, and being worshipped by all. But this outward semblance is a mystery. In reality they are beasts which have ascended from the pit one after another to overthrow the order of God. But this order, which is another mystery, has always opposed to them really great and powerful men who have dealt these monsters a mortal wound. As fast as hell vomits them forth, Heaven at the same time creates fresh heroes to combat them. Ancient history, sacred and profane, is but a record of this war. The order of God has ever remained victorious and those who have ranged themselves on the side of God have shared His triumph, and are happy for all eternity.

A CATALOG OF SELECTED DOVER
BOOKS IN ALL FIELDS OF INTEREST

CONCERNING THE SPIRITUAL IN ART, Wassily Kandinsky. Pioneering work by father of abstract art. Thoughts on color theory, nature of art. Analysis of earlier masters. 12 illustrations. 80pp. of text. 5⅜ x 8½.   0-486-23411-8

CELTIC ART: The Methods of Construction, George Bain. Simple geometric techniques for making Celtic interlacements, spirals, Kells-type initials, animals, humans, etc. Over 500 illustrations. 160pp. 9 x 12. (Available in U.S. only.)   0-486-22923-8

AN ATLAS OF ANATOMY FOR ARTISTS, Fritz Schider. Most thorough reference work on art anatomy in the world. Hundreds of illustrations, including selections from works by Vesalius, Leonardo, Goya, Ingres, Michelangelo, others. 593 illustrations. 192pp. 7⅛ x 10¼.   0-486-20241-0

CELTIC HAND STROKE-BY-STROKE (Irish Half-Uncial from "The Book of Kells"): An Arthur Baker Calligraphy Manual, Arthur Baker. Complete guide to creating each letter of the alphabet in distinctive Celtic manner. Covers hand position, strokes, pens, inks, paper, more. Illustrated. 48pp. 8¼ x 11.   0-486-24336-2

EASY ORIGAMI, John Montroll. Charming collection of 32 projects (hat, cup, pelican, piano, swan, many more) specially designed for the novice origami hobbyist. Clearly illustrated easy-to-follow instructions insure that even beginning papercrafters will achieve successful results. 48pp. 8¼ x 11.   0-486-27298-2

BLOOMINGDALE'S ILLUSTRATED 1886 CATALOG: Fashions, Dry Goods and Housewares, Bloomingdale Brothers. Famed merchants' extremely rare catalog depicting about 1,700 products: clothing, housewares, firearms, dry goods, jewelry, more. Invaluable for dating, identifying vintage items. Also, copyright-free graphics for artists, designers. Co-published with Henry Ford Museum & Greenfield Village. 160pp. 8¼ x 11.   0-486-25780-0

THE ART OF WORLDLY WISDOM, Baltasar Gracian. "Think with the few and speak with the many," "Friends are a second existence," and "Be able to forget" are among this 1637 volume's 300 pithy maxims. A perfect source of mental and spiritual refreshment, it can be opened at random and appreciated either in brief or at length. 128pp. 5⅜ x 8½.   0-486-44034-6

JOHNSON'S DICTIONARY: A Modern Selection, Samuel Johnson (E. L. McAdam and George Milne, eds.). This modern version reduces the original 1755 edition's 2,300 pages of definitions and literary examples to a more manageable length, retaining the verbal pleasure and historical curiosity of the original. 480pp. 5³⁄₁₆ x 8¼. 0-486-44089-3

ADVENTURES OF HUCKLEBERRY FINN, Mark Twain, Illustrated by E. W. Kemble. A work of eternal richness and complexity, a source of ongoing critical debate, and a literary landmark, Twain's 1885 masterpiece about a barefoot boy's journey of self-discovery has enthralled readers around the world. This handsome clothbound reproduction of the first edition features all 174 of the original black-and-white illustrations. 368pp. 5⅜ x 8½.   0-486-44322-1

CATALOG OF DOVER BOOKS

MAKING FURNITURE MASTERPIECES: 30 Projects with Measured Drawings, Franklin H. Gottshall. Step-by-step instructions, illustrations for constructing handsome, useful pieces, among them a Sheraton desk, Chippendale chair, Spanish desk, Queen Anne table and a William and Mary dressing mirror. 224pp. 8⅛ x 11¼.
0-486-29338-6

NORTH AMERICAN INDIAN DESIGNS FOR ARTISTS AND CRAFTSPEOPLE, Eva Wilson. Over 360 authentic copyright-free designs adapted from Navajo blankets, Hopi pottery, Sioux buffalo hides, more. Geometrics, symbolic figures, plant and animal motifs, etc. 128pp. 8⅜ x 11. (Not for sale in the United Kingdom.)   0-486-25341-4

THE FOSSIL BOOK: A Record of Prehistoric Life, Patricia V. Rich et al. Profusely illustrated definitive guide covers everything from single-celled organisms and dinosaurs to birds and mammals and the interplay between climate and man. Over 1,500 illustrations. 760pp. 7½ x 10⅛.   0-486-29371-8

VICTORIAN ARCHITECTURAL DETAILS: Designs for Over 700 Stairs, Mantels, Doors, Windows, Cornices, Porches, and Other Decorative Elements, A. J. Bicknell & Company. Everything from dormer windows and piazzas to balconies and gable ornaments. Also includes elevations and floor plans for handsome, private residences and commercial structures. 80pp. 9⅜ x 12¼.   0-486-44015-X

WESTERN ISLAMIC ARCHITECTURE: A Concise Introduction, John D. Hoag. Profusely illustrated critical appraisal compares and contrasts Islamic mosques and palaces–from Spain and Egypt to other areas in the Middle East. 139 illustrations. 128pp. 6 x 9.   0-486-43760-4

CHINESE ARCHITECTURE: A Pictorial History, Liang Ssu-ch'eng. More than 240 rare photographs and drawings depict temples, pagodas, tombs, bridges, and imperial palaces comprising much of China's architectural heritage. 152 halftones, 94 diagrams. 232pp. 10¾ x 9⅞.   0-486-43999-2

THE RENAISSANCE: Studies in Art and Poetry, Walter Pater. One of the most talked-about books of the 19th century, *The Renaissance* combines scholarship and philosophy in an innovative work of cultural criticism that examines the achievements of Botticelli, Leonardo, Michelangelo, and other artists. "The holy writ of beauty."–Oscar Wilde. 160pp. 5⅜ x 8½.   0-486-44025-7

A TREATISE ON PAINTING, Leonardo da Vinci. The great Renaissance artist's practical advice on drawing and painting techniques covers anatomy, perspective, composition, light and shadow, and color. A classic of art instruction, it features 48 drawings by Nicholas Poussin and Leon Battista Alberti. 192pp. 5⅜ x 8½.
0-486-44155-5

THE MIND OF LEONARDO DA VINCI, Edward McCurdy. More than just a biography, this classic study by a distinguished historian draws upon Leonardo's extensive writings to offer numerous demonstrations of the Renaissance master's achievements, not only in sculpture and painting, but also in music, engineering, and even experimental aviation. 384pp. 5⅜ x 8½.   0-486-44142-3

WASHINGTON IRVING'S RIP VAN WINKLE, Illustrated by Arthur Rackham. Lovely prints that established artist as a leading illustrator of the time and forever etched into the popular imagination a classic of Catskill lore. 51 full-color plates. 80pp. 8⅜ x 11.   0-486-44242-X

HENSCHE ON PAINTING, John W. Robichaux. Basic painting philosophy and methodology of a great teacher, as expounded in his famous classes and workshops on Cape Cod. 7 illustrations in color on covers. 80pp. 5⅜ x 8½.   0-486-43728-0

CATALOG OF DOVER BOOKS

LIGHT AND SHADE: A Classic Approach to Three-Dimensional Drawing, Mrs. Mary P. Merrifield. Handy reference clearly demonstrates principles of light and shade by revealing effects of common daylight, sunshine, and candle or artificial light on geometrical solids. 13 plates. 64pp. $5\frac{3}{8}$ x $8\frac{1}{2}$. 0-486-44143-1

ASTROLOGY AND ASTRONOMY: A Pictorial Archive of Signs and Symbols, Ernst and Johanna Lehner. Treasure trove of stories, lore, and myth, accompanied by more than 300 rare illustrations of planets, the Milky Way, signs of the zodiac, comets, meteors, and other astronomical phenomena. 192pp. $8\frac{3}{8}$ x 11. 0-486-43981-X

JEWELRY MAKING: Techniques for Metal, Tim McCreight. Easy-to-follow instructions and carefully executed illustrations describe tools and techniques, use of gems and enamels, wire inlay, casting, and other topics. 72 line illustrations and diagrams. 176pp. $8\frac{1}{4}$ x $10\frac{7}{8}$. 0-486-44043-5

MAKING BIRDHOUSES: Easy and Advanced Projects, Gladstone Califf. Easy-to-follow instructions include diagrams for everything from a one-room house for bluebirds to a forty-two-room structure for purple martins. 56 plates; 4 figures. 80pp. $8\frac{3}{4}$ x $6\frac{3}{8}$. 0-486-44183-0

LITTLE BOOK OF LOG CABINS: How to Build and Furnish Them, William S. Wicks. Handy how-to manual, with instructions and illustrations for building cabins in the Adirondack style, fireplaces, stairways, furniture, beamed ceilings, and more. 102 line drawings. 96pp. $8\frac{3}{4}$ x $6\frac{3}{8}$. 0-486-44259-4

THE SEASONS OF AMERICA PAST, Eric Sloane. From "sugaring time" and strawberry picking to Indian summer and fall harvest, a whole year's activities described in charming prose and enhanced with 79 of the author's own illustrations. 160pp. $8\frac{1}{4}$ x 11. 0-486-44220-9

THE METROPOLIS OF TOMORROW, Hugh Ferriss. Generous, prophetic vision of the metropolis of the future, as perceived in 1929. Powerful illustrations of towering structures, wide avenues, and rooftop parks–all features in many of today's modern cities. 59 illustrations. 144pp. $8\frac{1}{4}$ x 11. 0-486-43727-2

THE PATH TO ROME, Hilaire Belloc. This 1902 memoir abounds in lively vignettes from a vanished time, recounting a pilgrimage on foot across the Alps and Apennines in order to "see all Europe which the Christian Faith has saved." 77 of the author's original line drawings complement his sparkling prose. 272pp. $5\frac{3}{8}$ x $8\frac{1}{2}$. 0-486-44001-X

THE HISTORY OF RASSELAS: Prince of Abissinia, Samuel Johnson. Distinguished English writer attacks eighteenth-century optimism and man's unrealistic estimates of what life has to offer. 112pp. $5\frac{3}{8}$ x $8\frac{1}{2}$. 0-486-44094-X

A VOYAGE TO ARCTURUS, David Lindsay. A brilliant flight of pure fancy, where wild creatures crowd the fantastic landscape and demented torturers dominate victims with their bizarre mental powers. 272pp. $5\frac{3}{8}$ x $8\frac{1}{2}$. 0-486-44198-9

Paperbound unless otherwise indicated. Available at your book dealer, online at **www.doverpublications.com**, or by writing to Dept. GI, Dover Publications, Inc., 31 East 2nd Street, Mineola, NY 11501. For current price information or for free catalogs (please indicate field of interest), write to Dover Publications or log on to **www.doverpublications.com** and see every Dover book in print. Dover publishes more than 500 books each year on science, elementary and advanced mathematics, biology, music, art, literary history, social sciences, and other areas.